SAMSUNG GALAXY NOTE 20 & 20 ULTRA

USER'S GUIDE

A well explanatory and comprehensive user's guide to master the new Samsung Galaxy Note 20 series from beginner to professional level

MICHAEL

JOSH

Copyright

Printed in the United States of America
© 2019 by Michael Josh

Churchgate Publishing House

USA | UK | Canada

Table of Contents

Why This Guide?

So, are you happy or what?

Glad you are a proud owner of the trendy Samsung Galaxy Note 20/20 ultra. Or probably you got this book in anticipation of getting one (Samsung Galaxy Note 20 series) or receiving it as a gift. Whichever way, thanks, and it is my pleasure for you reading *Samsung Galaxy Note 20 and 20 Ultra User's Guide.* With this simple and illustrated guide with step-by-step instructions, handy tips, and trick, clearer images, you have got in mind to learn everything you need about the Samsung Galaxy Note 20 series. This book will give insight into its premium features and some hidden tricks and tips. It will also help to get the best out of your new device.

About the Author

Michael josh is a tech explorer with over 12 years of experience in the ICT sector. He developed himself with his advancement in information communication technology, which facilitates his writing skills. His hobby is exploring new things and fixing problems in its most straightforward form has been his focus ever since. Michael obtained a Bachelor's and a Master's Degree in Computer Science and Information Communication Technology from New Jersey Institute of Technology Newark, NJ.

Chapter 1

Samsung Galaxy Note series-A history of innovation

Introduction

So, when Samsung introduced the first galaxy note, they received many criticisms from the mainstream media for its gigantic size. Such as *"The note is so big, it needs its zip code," "I need to show you my new phone," "That's ridiculous," "Samsung has no idea of what they are doing," "This is like talking into a piece of toast" "people called it **Phablet**" "Skip over the Samsung galaxy note completely."* But the company let people know they're going to change the platform of the phone in history.

Samsung Galaxy Note

It can be deduced from the fact that large screen phones have become so common that the whole tablet has lost its relevance. Even the apple that criticized Samsung for their big phones, is now making big display smartphones themselves. It was said with the latest announcement of the Samsung galaxy note 20 just a few weeks ago. Let's take a look at how the galaxy note has evolved over the years, which single-handedly kick-started the trend of large screen phones, which is a norm these days.

$\mathcal{S}$amsung Galaxy Note

Samsung released the first galaxy note back in September 2011. It was the first top android device to spot with a stylus pen and had a 5.3-inch display, which was considered gigantic back then. Top of the line specs as well with enhance hardware in technology wasn't as good as it is now. So, it is understandable.

Do you know the interesting thing? Guess!. Even with all the criticism and quarrelling, the galaxy note was in a standard that sold over 10 million units in the first year alone, which gave them the confidence to launch a series of devices in the years to come.

$\mathcal{S}$amsung Galaxy Note real facts

- The 5.3-inch display was one of the largest back then
- Other regions had the Exynos 4210 chipset while North America had the Qualcomm Snapdragon S3

- The phone was shipped with an Android version 2.3 and stop support at Android version 4.1
- The S pen with 256 levels of pressure sensitivity introduced first

Samsung Galaxy Note 2

After the success of the original Galaxy Note, Samsung simply had to release a redefined successor. The Galaxy Note two also improved upon every aspect. The design inspired by Galaxy S3 and added quite impressive spec sheets as well.

Samsung perfected the area in which the first galaxy note was underperforming. The device came with an improved battery capacity with an improved Quad-core processor. The S pen was also improved, the camera produced some of the outstanding images back then, and it also adds an HD super AMOLED display.

All in all, what the Galaxy Note started, the Galaxy Note two push it to a greater extent.

Samsung Galaxy Note 2 real facts

- The Note 2 debuted the air view feature, which allows you to preview content by hovering the pen
- The pressure sensitivity of the S pen increased to 1024 levels for better accuracy
- A split-screen feature was introduced to the phone which let you display two apps at a time

Samsung Galaxy Note 3 & Neo

With the galaxy note three, Samsung showcase the new design language at that time. Samsung stepped up the design prowess to make it fancier to the business users. The hardware on the device was the best we could have at that time. The faux brush aluminum looks with faux leather on the back, bringing the latest premium next to the answered. It has grown up in size at a 5.7-inch 1080p display.

Samsung Galaxy Note 3
Released September, 2013 - $650

ANDROID 4.3 | EXYNOS 5420 | AMOLED DISPLAY

DISPLAY **5.7"**

CAMERAS **13MP** FRONT 2MP

INTERNAL STORAGE **16/32/64GB** MICROSDXC

RAM **3GB**

BATTERY **3200** mAh

WEIGHT **168g**

The camera, for the first time, was able to record 4k videos and had the best specs you could have at that time.

Samsung Galaxy Note 3 Neo
Released February, 2014 - $550

ANDROID 4.3 | EXYNOS 5250 | AMOLED DISPLAY

DISPLAY **5.5"**

CAMERAS **8MP** FRONT 2MP

INTERNAL STORAGE **16GB** MICROSDXC

RAM **2GB**

BATTERY **3100** mAh

WEIGHT **162g**

They also released a turned down version of the Note 3-the, galaxy note three (3) Neo, which had mid-range specs and intended for the imaging market. Over 10 million units of the Note 3 sold in the first two months to make it one of the best-selling premium devices in 2013.

Talking about the S pen, it got a major feature update and the air command menu that works like the usual PC mouse to the right-click button.

Samsung Galaxy Note 3 real facts

- The phone was the first device to ship with 3GB of RAM
- It featured a full HD 1080p display and a bigger screen display
- Its design was a mix of faux metal and plastic leather

Samsung Galaxy Note 4 & Edge

The Note 4 is the same old Galaxy winning formula perfected as much as it gets. The Note series is already getting its stand in the big-screen smartphone market. The outstanding performance, large screen size, and the handy S pen features had made it a top dog.

It has a Quad-HD display with gorilla glass four, making it one the best displays as of that time. Also, the body design was coupled with a metal frame bringing the world premium next to the answer. The series features its first fingerprint reader on the home screen button and an improved camera of the 16-mega pixel. Samsung came up with health initiatives with a pulse oximeter and heart-rate monitor integrated on the back of the phone.

Note 4 featured Optical Image Stabilization (OIS), which is taken for levity hand nowadays. OIS is a technology that monitors the camera lens movement.

Anytime a camera integrated with Optical Image Stabilization takes a photo, the picture is captured in a period. When working with ample light, the period is extremely short but longer in low light.

The Note 4 S pen pressure sensitivity was doubled to 2048 levels, which allows a better approach to managing drawing on the device.

However, the Samsung Galaxy Note series gained ground as one of the best-selling devices and part of their flagship lineup.

Samsung unveiled a device with a display curved at one side and called it **the galaxy note four edges.** The spec sheet of the Note 4 and Edge are similar. The curved edge can be used as shortcuts to a different application. More so, the curved edge includes a sidebar that can be used to access and display different panels.

Samsung Galaxy Note Edge
Released November, 2014 · $950

ANDROID 4.4.4 · SNAPDRAGON 805 · AMOLED DISPLAY · FINGERPRINT

DISPLAY 5.6"

CAMERAS 16MP FRONT 3.7MP

INTERNAL STORAGE 32/64GB MICROSDXC

RAM 3GB

BATTERY 3000 mAh FAST CHARGE 15W

WEIGHT 174g

GALAXY Note Edge

My Galaxy Note Edge

A device with such an intricate form pattern quickly became the norm in all the Samsung flagship devices in the year to come. With the Note 4 edge, Samsung proved the critics wrong and gave a message that they are at the forefront of smartphone innovation.

Samsung Galaxy Note 4 real facts

- The S pen level upgraded to 2048
- The design was changed from a faux metal frame to aluminum
- An ultraviolet (UV) ray measurement was integrated to monitor the heart-rate and the SpO2 (oxygen saturation) sensor
- The Note 4 edge was the first phone to ship with a curved edge
- The Note 4 edge was debuted as the "Youm" concept phone at CES 2013

Samsung Galaxy Note 5

The Samsung Galaxy Note 5 was released in 2015 to mark the company's annual refresh cycle. The phone was coupled with major hardware back then, which made greater improvements in all.

Samsung Galaxy Note 5
Released August, 2015 - $700

ANDROID 5.1.1 | EXYNOS 7420 | AMOLED DISPLAY | FINGERPRINT

DISPLAY
5.7"

CAMERAS
16MP
FRONT 5MP

INTERNAL STORAGE
32/64/128GB
NO CARD SLOT

RAM
4GB

BATTERY
3000 mAh
FAST CHARGE 15W

WEIGHT
171g

Note 5 saw a big design change. Samsung used the glass and metal design that looks good. It also makes some sacrifices; the micro SD slot was missing. There was no removable battery, and they dished out IR blaster. Also, the company didn't sell Note 5 in Europe for some reason. It was a great phone, nevertheless, but it split the fan base, and a lot of loyal Samsung fans were unhappy with the desertion Samsung made with the Galaxy Note 5.

Samsung Galaxy Note 5 real facts

- The Galaxy Note 5 debuted the non-removable batteries on the Note series
- The Note 5 also debuted the spring-loaded stylus
- It was the first time on the series with glass design

Samsung Galaxy Note 7

As we all know, the next figure after Note 5 should be 6. NO! Samsung made this decision to Note 7 not to bring confusion to their fans with the S series being ahead with a figure that year.

From now on, the Note and S series receive equivalent model numbers.

The fans were not happy with the sacrifice done on Note 5, but Samsung couldn't get away with it. So, Samsung quickly learned the lesson and brought back the micro SD slot, the expandable storage. It inherited the curved display on the Galaxy Note 4 edge, but this time around, it was a dual-curved edges display. Due to the first time of dual-curved display, the curvature wasn't something dramatic.

With Note 7, the S pen also improved with an IP68 rating and got a major upgrade with some special features like translating texts, record GIFs, and a screen magnifier. The new-fangled scanner was upgraded to Samsung pass for secure payments.

Note 7 was the best smartphone ever made, with a massive upgrade to the series. The demand for the phone was high then, with it broken the pre-order numbers in Samsung's home market (South Korea).

Not long after the release of the phone in August 2016, users started complaining about the phone being overheating and even exploding. However, Samsung acted fast on these issues then hasten up and released another revised Note 7 of the initial one. Yet, the new version still catches fire, and the company had to pull down the just-released version two months after.

Samsung Galaxy Note FE
Released July, 2017 - $600

In mid-2017, Samsung refurbished Note 7 models with fair battery capacity to the previous Note 7 versions in selected countries in Asia under the Galaxy Note fan edition branding (Galaxy Note 7 SE). It was the version among the series that debuted Samsung's Bixby digital assistant.

Samsung Galaxy Note 7 real facts

- The Samsung Galaxy Note 7 featured infrared-base recognition for secure unlocking
- The refurbished Note 7 featured a fewer battery capacity and new safety features

- The refurbished Note 7 was named Samsung Galaxy Note 7 FE (fan edition)
- The phone was shipped to customers with fireproof boxes for the safe return
- A software update was rolled out to the Note 7 to deactivate its functionality completely

Samsung Galaxy Note 8

Following the fiasco faced on Note 7, Samsung came up with Note 8. This time around, they played it safe and avoided the debacle of Note 7 by reducing the battery capacity.

Samsung Galaxy Note 8
Released August, 2017 - $950

ANDROID 7.1.1 | EXYNOS 8895 | AMOLED DISPLAY | FINGERPRINT | IP68 CERTIFICATION

DISPLAY 6.3"

CAMERAS 12+12MP FRONT 8+2MP

INTERNAL STORAGE 64/128/256GB MICROSDXC

RAM 6GB

BATTERY 3300 mAh FAST CHARGE 15W

WEIGHT 195g

The phone featured a 6.3-inch display, Exynos 8895, and the dual-curved edge from Note 7. The first time the series will feature dual camera-A 12-mega pixel and a 12-mega pixel telephoto lens. The phone debuted the **Dex** feature, which allows the usage of Note 8 as a computer when connected into a keyboard and monitor.

Even with the pressure the company faced with Note 7, regardless of the overall improvements to the phone, the Note 8 sold over a total number of 270,000 units on the first weekend of sales.

Samsung Galaxy Note 8 real facts

- The Galaxy Note 8 featured a dedicated key for Bixby virtual assistant
- It was the first Note series to feature a dual-lens camera
- The refreshed camera app is used to adjust the intensity of background-blur before and after capturing the image
- The 'screen-off memo' feature allows you to add a note directly to the locked home screen

Samsung Galaxy Note 9

The Galaxy Note 9 didn't have many changes as it had the same design as the Note 8 but saw a lot of improvement internally and had some of the amazing specs of 2018. However, that doesn't mean the Note 9 is lacking behind with a few new features. The phone was the first Samsung phone to featured up to 8GB of RAM and 512GB of ROM. Also, it came with the top of the line chipset.

Samsung Galaxy Note 9
Released August, 2018 - $1,000

ANDROID 8.1 | EXYNOS 9810 | AMOLED DISPLAY | FINGERPRINT? | IP68 CERTIFICATION

DISPLAY
6.4"

CAMERAS
12+12MP
FRONT 8+2MP

INTERNAL STORAGE
128/512GB
MICROSDXC

RAM
6/8GB

BATTERY
4000 mAh
FAST CHARGE 15W

WEIGHT
201g

The S pen was the high line as it got many new features such as the Bluetooth capabilities and a built-in battery.

With the S pen, it can be used as a shortcut for actions and to move backward and forward.

The slow in innovation see Note 9 had small sales with 9.6 million lowers than Note 8, and it also affects the rate of demand for Samsung's premium devices.

Samsung Galaxy Note 9 real facts

- The S-pen was made of a built-in battery that charges via the housing provided for the S-pen at the bottom of the phone

- 40 seconds charge is enough for 30 minutes used of the battery

- The Galaxy Note 9 debuted the 8GB of RAM in Samsung devices

- Note 9 made the farewell to the headphone jack in the Note series

Samsung Galaxy Note 10 series

With the smartphone market flooded with large screen devices, Samsung made the pivotal decision. For the first time, the Samsung Note series came in two versions globally. Note 10 and the Note 10 plus. Everything about the phone was great; the looks, the camera, the displays. Except it was the first time, Samsung flagship doesn't have a headphone jack. Both devices made Samsung target two markets and price segments, a smart move after the disappointing sales of Note 9.

Talking about the display of the two models, they both came with an AMOLED display with dynamic tone mapping for better color accuracy. The Note 10 plus was a bit taller to Note 10 as it featured a 19:9 aspect ratio. However, the smaller model came with a 6.3-inch Full HD display with trimmed down physical dimensions.

To make a difference between the models, Samsung coupled the Note 10 plus with a higher battery capacity of 4300mAh, which could be charged up to 45W, while the Note 10 was coupled with a high battery 3500mAh with 25W capacity.

Samsung Galaxy Note 10+
Released August, 2019 - $1099

ANDROID 9.0 · EXYNOS 9825 · AMOLED DISPLAY · FINGERPRINT · IP68 CERTIFICATION

DISPLAY 6.8"
CAMERAS 12+12+16+0.3MP FRONT 10MP
INTERNAL STORAGE 256/512GB MICROSDXC
RAM 12GB
BATTERY 4300 mAh FAST CHARGE 45W
WEIGHT 196g

As usual, the S pen came with some new features as well. Samsung included a gyroscope inside the pen, which lets users do plenty of things like; changing the camera mode, zooming on the pictures, controlling playback on YouTube, or skipping through images, songs, or videos. Also, the Samsung Note 10 series could convert handwriting into text, and there were AR doodles. All in all, the Galaxy Note 10 plus was one of the best Galaxy Note, in my opinion.

Samsung Galaxy Note 10 (series) real facts

- The phone integrated the power button to the Bixby button, but there is room to change it back
- The debuted the Infinity-O display with a selfie camera cut-out

- A sub-version called Note 10 Lite was introduced with a few changes in specs but maintain the fast charging, stylus input, and a headphone jack
- The S pen featured a gyroscope for remote control

Chapter 2

What's inside the box?

Here it is a black box as per usual. With the label, "N20" printed upfront just as it was on the S20 series box. Anyhow, from the color of the S Pen, you can probably tell the color of the phone that you have inside.

Go ahead and open it up. You have got the usual bits inside the box coming from the quick reference guide, terms and condition note, and Samsung care note follow by the sim card tool, a USB Type-C to USB Type-C cable, and some AKG USB type-C earphones as well as a 25W fast charger adapter.

Normally, you do get some nibs for the S pen and a removing tool, but the company took it off this time around. Mind you, what is inside the box varies depending on your country. Like in the USA, Samsung said they would not be bundling the usual AKG earphone with the device. Probably a way to encourage people to get the new Galaxy Buds live.

Chapter 3

Device specifications

Difference between Note 20 regular and Ultra

	NOTE 20 REGULAR	NOTE 20 ULTRA
Build (back)	Gorilla glass VICTUS	polycarbonate
Build (front)	Gorilla glass VICTUS	Gorilla glass 5
Design	Sharp angular corner	Sharp angular corner
Display	Samsung curved display	Samsung flat display
Screen	Dynamic AMOLED QHD+ 120Hz	Super AMOLED plus FHD+ 60Hz
RAM	12GB	8GB
ROM	128GB NO SD slot	128/512GB SD slot available up to 1TB
Battery capacity	4300mAh	4500mAh
S-pen latency	26ms	9ms
Front camera	10MP f/2.2	10MP f/2.2
Rear camera	64MP f/1.8 WIDE/12MP 120° UWA/ 12MP 3x Telephoto	108MP f/1.8 WIDE/12MP 120° UWA/ 12MP 5x Telephoto

Display

It is really difficult not to take to the display of a high-end Samsung phone. The Note 20 series has one of the best displays you can get on a phone today. And for the spec upset, you will be happy on this Note 20, unlike last year's Note 10 display.

The large 6.9-inch make it the biggest note to date. It is a dynamic AMOLED display 2x panel, which means you can choose a WQHD+ resolution with the regular 60 Hz refresh rate or a full FHD+ resolution with the 120 Hz refresh rate. In contrast to the N20 Ultra, the 120 Hz refresh rate is part of an adaptive mode that dynamically adjusts the refresh rate depending on what you are doing in other to save on battery.

Display
HDR10+ / 120Hz

For example, if you are watching a 30fps video, you won't benefit from the screen refreshing 120 times per second. So, it will switch to 60 Hz when you don't touch the phone for a few seconds, but it will go for 120 Hz for support games. For the major situations, this does work well but doesn't perfect.

Well, the screen very shines, its brightness like eligibility. It measures 1024nits with the adaptive brightness in broad daylight.

Display
Shown in direct sunlight

But if you want to adjust it manually, the Note 20 ultra offered up to 500nits, which is impressive. The screen is the brightest AMOLED screen we've seen to date. The display also supports HDR10+, which makes the color outlook quite satisfying.

The natural mode had favored the production while the vivid mode was less accurate but nice in punchy.

Love it or hate it, the Note 20 series kicked Samsung signature curved display.

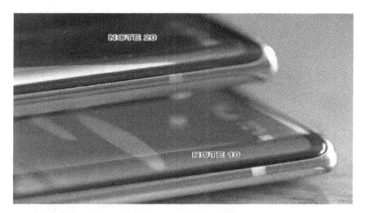

It doesn't slope as much as on the Note 10, making it less intrusive and making it less acceptable to tap accidentally. I don't mind it, but I can see why a flat slab will make more sense for a device made as a note-taking device.

There is an ultrasonic scanner big underneath, which is fast and reliable.

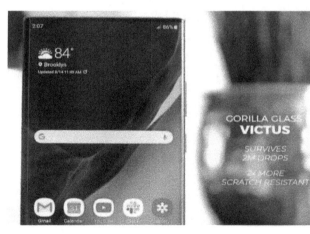

Also, it is the first phone to use corning new gorilla glass technology called **victus,** which supposedly can survive 2-meter drops without shattering and 2x more scratch resistant.

Design

The Galaxy Note 20 ultra continues the sharp corner legacy of its predecessors but in a more refined style. On the outside edge, there is the volume rocker and the power sleep/wake button below it.

The bottom of the phone comprises of the microphone, speaker, the USB Type-C charging port, and the S pen. While on the top, there is the sim card tray and another microphone

The line defining color is the mystic brown this year, which is much more than the note series in the past. The color has a gentle-looking mark finish on the back, and It doesn't pick the fingerprint easily.

Turn the phone around, and you will see a massive screen with extremely tiny bezels, and a very small center opened at the top of the phone. Unfortunately, you will find the same ultrasonic fingerprint we see before, far from being the fastest onscreen fingerprint in the phone market.

Battery and capacity

The phone has a 4500mAh battery, which is 10% smaller than the one on the S20 Ultra. Nevertheless, it got the same core time and standby performance, which included Samsung produce optimization.

What surprises, however, is that the Note 20 ultra got an improved battery life in the web browsing test. So, we can speculate the new panel is more power-efficient when showing predominantly light content. The biggest surprise was that we didn't see any meaningful improvement in the playback test.

4500mAh battery
25W fast charging for a full charge in about an hour

Despite the fact, the screen adapts to the adaptive mode and lower the refresh rate to 60 Hz whenever you have a full-screen video. The note 20 ultra performs equally well better than the S20 Ultra, but it is not due to the adaptive screen refresh rate, which doesn't appear to bring any battery life improvement.

There must be a factor that plays under the hold, but we can only guess what they are. Charging on Galaxy note 20 ultra is rated at 25W. With the provided charger, you will get 0-40% with half an hour, decent but 50% that Samsung promised.

Processor

The Note 20 ultra has the upgraded snapdragon 865+ chipset in North America and some parts of Asia. Everywhere else or Europe has the same Exynos 990 as where you find on the Galaxy S20 phones earlier this year (2020). I'm bump to see the gap between the two variant versions getting grinder than it used to be. Not only is then the upgrade of the Exynos module potential, the substantial advantage of the snapdragon version and battery life and performance.

The phone uses One UI on top of Android 10. If you're switching from other Galaxy phones, you will find this cleaner and easier to navigate with one hand. But if you are upgrading from another device with one UI, especially the 2.1 version, you won't see any major difference.

The edge panel has refined, the apps now larger, and the panel name moved to the middle.

Camera

The Note 20 ultra has a triple camera setup, which is different from what is on the S20 Ultra, although not entirely so. There is the main camera with a large sensor, ultrawide angle, and Telephoto with the periscope lens.

The main camera of the 108-megapixel sensor is the same as the one you can find on the Galaxy S20. It has an f/1.8 lens, the last of the variable aperture of some Galaxy flagship in the Past. The 12-megapixel ultra-wide, the f/2.2 aperture, is also the same as the S20 series.

Camera
12 MP / f/2.2 / 13mm lens

The telephoto zoom lens camera, on the other hand, is new, which came with a 12-megapixel, f/3.0 aperture, and a 120mm. Samsung has done away with the focus system they had on the S20 Ultra in favor of the laser system that works much better.

Camera
12 MP / f/3.0 / 120mm (periscope telephoto)

The selfie camera is 10-megapixel, capable of 4k 60p video shooting, and it also has autofocus takes very good photos that are improved better over the ones from Note 10 plus.

10MP
f/2.2 4K60P

Along with that, you can record 8k videos at 24fps (frame per second), and also, you can take 33-megapixel stills. It has a super lowlight camera capturing, and it can record super slow-motion in 720p 960fps

In most cases, you are normally shooting videos in 4k resolution. The camera comes out excellently from all the three cameras. You can also shoot 8k resolution from the main camera, this does offer more details than 4k, but the file size is massive.

Chapter 4

Setup your Galaxy Note 20 series

How to insert and remove the SIM/SD card

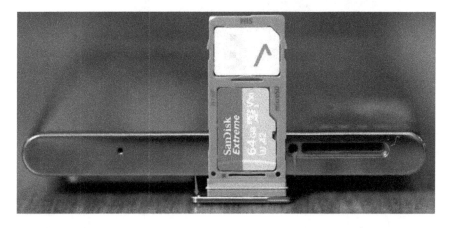

Now you have your Samsung Galaxy Note 20 series. Let's look at how to get a sim & SD card install on it.

The Note 20 ultra supports a SIM card and SD card, but the SD port can also be used for a second SIM card. While on the regular model, which is Note 20, doesn't support an SD card, which means it supports two sim cards.

How to Remove Sim tray

➤ Patiently grab your **SIM ejector** that came with your phone. If you don't have this, you can use another phone sim ejector

➤ Check the tiny hole on the left and not the microphone
➤ Insert the **SIM ejector** and give it a little bit pressure
➤ There is a small tiny lip, pull it out with your finger

Now, if you look at the tray on the Note 20 ultra, we have a port for the **SD card** and the other for a **nano-SIM card,** respectively.

How to insert the SIM card

Now, let's insert the **nano-SIM card**

➢ Make sure the hole for the pin is on the bottom right inside

- ➢ Now go ahead and grab your **nano-SIM card**
- ➢ Put and propel a little the **nano-SIM card** face-down in the smaller port, i.e., the port that goes inside of the device

You have learned how to remove the tray and how to insert the **nano-SIM card**. To insert the SD card is as simple as the **nano-SIM card.**

How to insert SD card

Now, let's insert the **SD card**

- ➢ Make sure the hole for the pin is on the bottom right inside
- ➢ Now go ahead and grab your **SD card**
- ➢ Put and propel a little the **SD card** face-down in the smaller port (Note 20 ultra only)

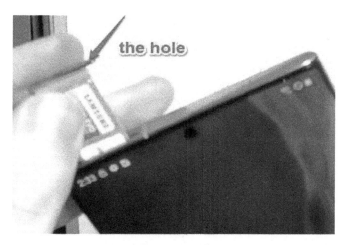

the hole

To remove the **nano-SIM/SD card,** follow the steps to remove the tray

Transfer data from the old device: Wireless method

Now let's turn on the phone and set up for the very first time.

Tap on the speaker logo at the top right corner to turn off the Bixby that talks as you set up the phone.

If you want voice guidance, make sure you enable the speaker logo.

Alright, tap on **"let's go"** to see the next interface. The first thing you are to do here is to select all the bullets options except for the optional one.

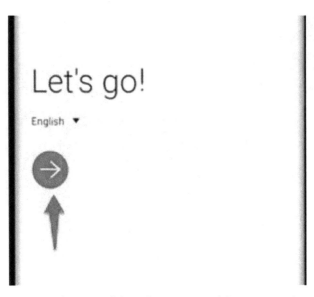

Click on **next**, and you will be shown to add a network.

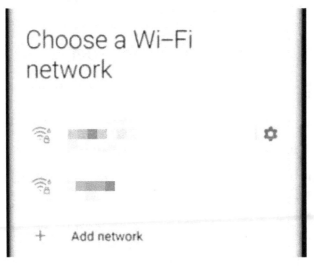

Turn off Wi-Fi

Connect your WIFI to the phone; if it requires a password, **input** your password, and **click** connect and if not, **click** connect to continue with the setup.

Now, the next thing is to **copy data** from your old device by tapping next or don't copy if you want to set up a brand-new device.

Don't copy

Before you can copy data from your old device, the very first thing you will do is download a **smart switch** on your old device from google store.

To continue with your old device data on your new Galaxy Note20 series, tap on **copy data**, wait for the device to update the **smart switch** on your new device. On the next screen, you will be asking how do you want to connect your devices. Do not fret; just tap on **wireless** and agree to the pop-up.

Open the **smart switch** on your old device to connect, tap on, agree, and allow all the permissions. On the next screen, tap on **send** to send data to your new device, then tap on **wireless,** and the two phones will communicate with one another. On your new device, select what **files** you want to copy from the old device. You can select everything or otherwise be specific on the files to copy, then scroll down on the new device and tap on **transfer.**

On your old device, tap on **copy,** then input your security to every command. On your new device, input the google account details on your old device, wait for verification, and all your account details will be **transferred** to your new device.

The next thing is to add your **Google account**, input your email and password, then click next. Wait for some seconds to fetch your account information from the server. Tap on next

Now let's see about **Google assistant**. You are all good to go. If your google account has already been set up, then click on more then accept for everything on google in row quick. And if you are yet to set it up, do read the information display and select your choices.

Transfer data from the old device: USB method

Not everyone will have access to the wireless transfer method, and transfer with the **USB cable** is also good. To transfer data from the old device with this method, you need a **USB type-**, a **smart switch** app, and also the **phone** you are copying the data. After you switch on your phone, tap on "**let's go**" as stated from the first method, agree to the **terms of service,** then tap on next. Connect to a **wireless** network, then tap **next** to continue with the setup. On the next interface, you will be asked if you want to copy data from your old device or start a new device. Now, tap on **next** to copy data from the old device.

Wait some minutes for the **smart switch** app to download updates; then, you select your old device type. Be it **Galaxy/Samsung** or **iPhone/iPad**. Agree on the pop-up after you select your phone type. An option is given on the next interface to select the type of data transfer to use. Tap on the **USB type** to proceed with the data transfer.

cable

wireless

The Note 20 series bundled with **USB Type-C** to **USB Type-C**. So, now grab your old phone and plug in the **USB cable** to its charging port and plug in the other side of the **USB** to your Samsung Galaxy Note 20 series.

After you have plugged in the **USB** to both devices, the same information as the one, this image will be displayed on your Samsung Galaxy Note 20 series, which is the new device you are transferring data.

Be calm enough and wait for both devices to connect.

The image above is the sample on how the interface should look when both devices are connected. The Pixel 4 XL is the old device, while Samsung is the new device. Exercise a little patient for the new device to scan all the files on the old device.

When the new device is done with the scanning, check on the new device to select what you will like to transfer from the old device to the new one.

After you selected your preferred files to transfer, scroll down on the same page, and tap on **"transfer."**

A pop-up will surface to select the time frame of the message to transfer. You can transfer all messages, and you can go as far and low as the last two years or last 30 days, respectively.

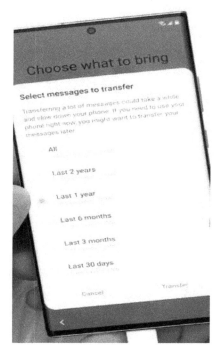

NOTE: *Transferring a lot of messages could take a while or slow down your device.*

If you want to make use of your device very soon, it is advisable not to **transfer** much of the messages. The whole message can be transferred later.

You can also bring back your google account to the new device. If you wish to bring your Google account, all you have to do is unlock your old device and tap on **"confirm."** And if you wish not to bring the google account over to the new device, just tap on **"skip."**

Do keep the cable connected while the data transfer is in progress. Then, disconnect it when the transfer is complete.

Let's set up the **fingerprints** or any security options as the data **transfer** is in progress.

Setup the fingerprints

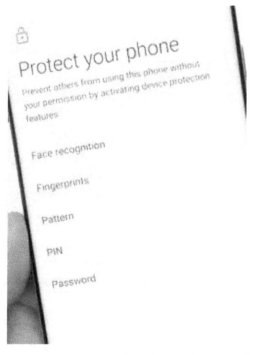

Though, the security section can be skipped as it will be discussed better in another chapter. The Galaxy Note 20 series featured the **ultrasonic fingerprint sensor**; in that case, ensure you have no screen protector on the screen. If there is any, do make sure it allows for the use of the **ultrasonic fingerprints sensor**.

➤ Go ahead and select **fingerprints** from the options

➤ Read the information and tap **"continue."**

- ➤ Before you can use a **fingerprint,** you need to activate any one of the following;
  - o Pattern
  - o Pin
  - o Password
- ➤ Select any of the security options above
- ➤ Input the required info, repeat this to confirm if the info matches each other
- ➤ Place and raise your thumb respectively on the assigned area for **fingerprint:**

With the **fingerprints** being set, log in to your Samsung account to finish up the setup. If you don't have a Samsung account, skip the step. You can create a Samsung account on their website.

Register the same fingerprints twice

Since the Galaxy Note 20 series is using the same ultrasonic sensor with the S20 series, it is going to help to speed up the process of scanning your fingerprint. The ultrasonic fingerprint sensor is more secure compare to other security options. Still, the downside of this is that sometimes it takes longer for your fingerprints to register with the scanner. So, doubling up on your fingerprints is going to help any issues that possibly could occur. Also, you can enable face recognition, but please be mindful it is not as secure as the fingerprint, pin, password, and pattern.

To register the fingerprints again, follow the below steps;

➢ Swipe down and tap the settings logo to access the phone settings

➢ Scroll down and select biometric and security

➢ Tap on fingerprints. Input your pin or other if it requires

➢ Tap on add fingerprints

➢ Then, go ahead and rescan the fingerprints you've already scan before

You can label your fingerprints to know exactly what fingers have been registered to your phone.

Just tap from the list of fingerprints, then you can input the custom name you want.

Chapter 5

Camera and its properties

Introduction to the device camera

Rebuilding the Samsung Galaxy Note 20 series camera from the ground up, even the N10 series camera was already great. The new N20 series smartphone is just pretty great and amazing.

There is a lot to talk about like larger image sensors that let in more light, the ability to zoom in the photo than before, 8K and 4K video capture, single take mode, and 33-megapixel screen capture from video.

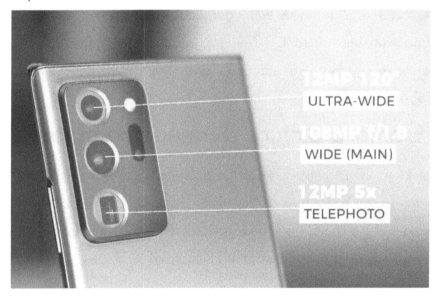

The N20 Ultra featured four cameras, including the 10-megapixel on the front. The hybrid zoom camera, 12-megapixel ultra-wide-angle camera, 108-megapixel wide (main), 3D-depth sensor camera, and a flash.

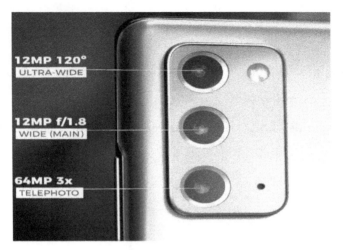

The N20 regular came with four cameras, including the 10-megapixels on the front, 12-megapixel ultra-wide camera, 12-megapixel wide-angle camera, and the 64-megapixel 3x telephoto camera.

Camera picture & video pro mode

The Note 20 ultra has one of the powerful Pro modes. You can switch to the pro mode or the menu mode by going into more sections of the camera and tapping the pro mode. In the pro mode, you will see a lot of custom options, which will be discussed below.

The ISO

 On the left-hand side, the first option you can find is the ISO, between 50 and 3200. ISO is the camera sensor sensitivity to light. The lower the ISO, the darker the image will appear, while the higher the **ISO,** the brighter the image. The highest **ISO** will also bring a higher amount of noise to the image. Typically, it is suggested to keep the **ISO** value low, which should rely more on the external light by taking the **ISO** in 1800.

For the best result, an **ISO** of 100 or 200 values with external light will do a great job.

The shutter speeds

 Next to ISO is the **shutter speed,** which simply means saturation for which the shadow of your camera remains open and let the light in. **Shutter speed** goes down to all the way 1/1200, and the maximum you can get is 30 seconds, which is quite much. The faster the **shutter speed** means the ability to fix some watching without blurring the background while the higher the **shutter speed** will let you capture many motions. For example, those light will or whatever your shots are capture by keeping the **shutter speed** high. You have to be very careful while tweaking the **shutter speed;** the ISO has to be mindful. For example, if you want to capture the light will or

whatever shots, you will probably keep the ISO value to 50 or 100, and the shutter speed will move between 4 or 5 seconds. Extremely low **shutter speed** can also be resulting in an extremely light image, while an extremely high can be resulting in an extremely light or a very poor image.

In physics, there is something called **exposure** that keeps adjusting your telephoto automatically. This **exposure** should be in the range of 0 and 1 only. Ensure that your **ISO** and **shutter speed** that keeps **the exposure** to 0 and 1 only.

The white balance

The white balance on the note 20 series ranges from 2300k to 10000k. The lower you go, the cooler the animate becomes, while the higher you go, the warmer it becomes. White balance should be something around 5000k, but you can change it according to the color that you need. White balance is originally used to remove the unrealistic always form on the image.

The standard

The standard is made for color adjustment. There are different categories for which color can be adjusted.

- ➢ Tint
- ➢ Contrast

- ➤ Saturation
- ➤ Highlight
- ➤ Shadow

The lower the value of the color adjustment, the lesser it effects, while the higher the value, the more in excess its effect. One has to be in between the value given, which ranges from 1-100. The adjustment settings can also be reset to its stock settings. Just tap the RESET `RESET` on the top left corner.

The metering options

Metering is an exciting option. It can adjust the **ISO, shutter speed,** and **exposure** by measuring the brightness of the subject. To measure brightness from different areas of the frame, you get three options with the centered-weighted metering being the first one.

- ➤ **Centered-weighted:** This exposes an image by taking an average from the center of the frame.

- ➤ **Matrix:** This exposes an image by taking the average of all the bright areas appearing in the camera frame. It creates a balance between the brighter and the darker areas of the image. It also happens to be one of the most commonly used metering options.

➤ **Spot:** This is useful for the portrait. You can take the exposure for a selected focus point. A red circle will determine where your focus point is.

The Frame

The camera frame can also be changed for a user to use the standard 12-megapixel more. You can change it to 16:9 or full.

One thing to keep in mind is that the camera on 108-megapixel resolution doesn't support PRO mode, and there is no option to turn it ON either.

Turn ON save RAW Copies

It allows users to save the raw copies of their images for future reference purposes. It is vital for people that use the camera of their phone as their business. This feature is turned off by default. To turn it on, follow the steps below.

- Tap on the camera settings [⚙] logo at the top of the screen

- Locate "save options" and tap on it

- Toggle the button that is Infront of "save RAW copies."

The video Pro mode also resides in the more section of the phone.

The Omni

 In the video Pro mode, the custom microphone is by default set to Omni, which will pick up the sound from all directions.

The Front

 The front allows the microphone to pick the sound from the front only. All sound coming from other directions will be neglected. It is very useful when the cameraman or somebody else has to contribute to the video without being captured.

The Rear

 It is best for capturing sound coming towards the back of the phone. All other sounds from another angle will not be recorded.

The USB

 The Note 20 series has the USB option to connect to an external mic. To use this feature, all you have to do is connect the USB cable to the external microphone.

All sound from the external mic will be recorded and not from the phone microphone.

The Bluetooth

 If you're having one of those Bluetooth microphones, this feature can be used. Switch ON the Bluetooth of the phone and the Bluetooth of the microphone. Connect both to record the sound from the Bluetooth microphone.

There is the **ISO** feature that works in the same manner similar to the photos and the **shutter speed** options, which is also the same as it was explained previously.

Also, there is the **auto, menu focus, white balance,** and there is room to adjust the colors of the videos.

The zoom options

In the pro video, you can zoom up to **5.0x or 10.0x** its last lens zooms, and after that, the digital zoom takes over.

The Camera frames

The 16:9 and the 21:9 frames will be interesting with an 8k supports. To select another video camera resolution, go to the camera settings and go to the Pro video size.

And from here, you can select a resolution starting from (UHB 3840x2160 @60fps, 30fps and 24fps), (FHD 1920x1080 @120fps, 60fps, 30fps and 24fps) and (HD 1280x720 @30fps).

How to hide the front camera

Samsung made the front camera cut-out tiny, but if the body is hidden behind the fake bezel, you can do that.

Open the settings, display, full-screen apps. At the top right corner, tap on the three dots, the menu to reveal the advance settings.

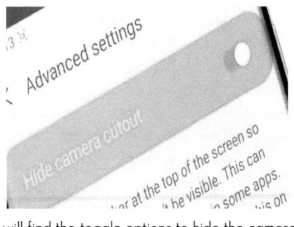

Here, you will find the toggle options to hide the camera. Switch it on, and it looks like it does not even there.

Connect 8KQLED TV and 8k video

capture

Finally, video capture also gets the same major upgrade. 8k video capture at 24 frames per secs is now possible.

Perfect view also has Samsung QLED 8K TV because now you have the device that shoots 8K contents that you can view on it and cast.

It is also now easier; all you have to do is tap your phone on the TV.

Pick moments from video in 33-megapixels

Now, because you are shooting a video in such a high resolution, the galaxy N20 series lets you pick your favorite moment on the same video and store as a 33-megapixels photo.

From the gallery app, just crop through the video and pick the frame that you like. You can also create a Gif file from the video.

How to move the shutter button on the screen

We have discussed the specifications of the camera in the last chapter. Now let check on how to handle its features.

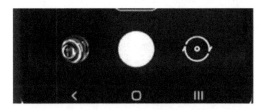

When you launch the camera, you have the shutter button at the bottom center of the screen, which may not be very convenient, especially based on how you handle your phone.

What you can do is that it is moveable to any part of the screen. All that you need is press hold and drag to anywhere on the screen for easy use.

When you are done with the camera, you can drag it back to its initial position.

Optical and hybrid zoom application

On the bottom of the camera box, these are the shortcut to jump around between the three lenses. The double middle tree , the icon is wide-angle, and the left three icons are the ultra-wide-angle, while the single three on the right is the telephoto.

At the bottom, you notice the addition zoom choice, which can be zoom up to 3x On the regular N20 but, N20 Ultra can be zoom up to 10x.

With so many zoom options, how does one get to the desire zoom point.? It is pretty easy, click any of the trees as mentioned, and on the side, you get options to pick the level of zoom.

Single take mode

Another nifty software features called **SINGLE TAKE MODE**. When a moment is taking place, and you can't quite figure it out if you want to take a photo or shoot a video, but with this feature, you can do both at a goal.

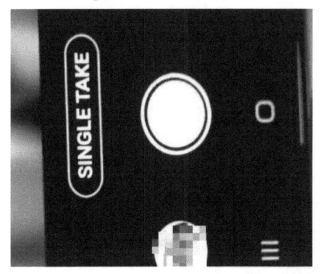

All you have to do is switch to the single take mode, and the phone will capture photos and video simultaneously for 10 seconds.

Once you are done, it will then offer you a curation of the best moment.

How to record 8k and 4k video

With the N20 series, you can shoot video at 8k and 4k quality. These allow the video to have a UHD display.

To record 8k or 4k video, dive into the camera settings by tapping the settings logo at the top left corner, scroll down to rear video size, and tap on it, and you have different sizes to capture videos.

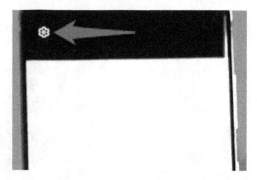

The first one is the 8k option, which video record is limited to 5 minutes.

The 4k option is seen under resolution.

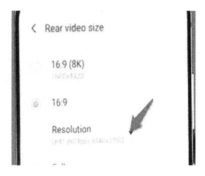

< Rear video size

16:9 (8K)

16:9

Resolution

These same features are available for the front camera.

Chapter 6

Enhance home screen display

Bring back the power button

By default, if you long-press the side-key, it launches the Bixby application. So, it is not possible to deliver the power off option display.

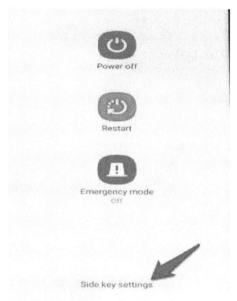

To turn off the phone, slide down the notification panel and tap on the power icon or go to the side key settings from the screen, then change the phone option for the side key to show the power off option when you long-press it.

Enable/disable gesture navigation

Again, by default, Samsung likes to employ its classic navigation buttons on the bottom of the screen, but if you go to the settings display follows by the navigation bar, you can enable full-screen gestures.

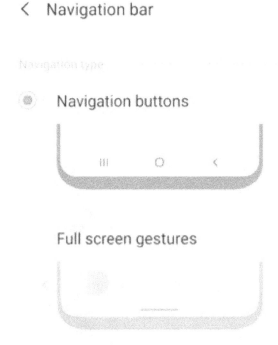

⟨   Navigation bar

Navigation type

◉   Navigation buttons

||| ○ ⟨

Full screen gestures

You can just swipe on the screen side to go back and swipe up on the screen to go home or swipe and hold to see the multitasking view on the screen. You can also disable this feature to use full-screen mode.

Getting more apps to your home screen

If you long-press the wallpaper on your home screen

you have the home screen settings at the bottom tap on it, and you see an option to change the home screen layout and number of rows and columns for applications.

Home screen grid
5X6

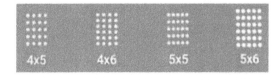

Choose the home screen grid option and select the layout that you want.

How to enable the percentage of battery

If, by default, the battery percentage isn't shown in the status bar, you can save the stress of swiping down the notification panel to check the battery meter.

2:38

Mon, March 2

Button order

Quick panel layout

Status bar

Status bar

Show notification icons

Number of notifications only

3 most recent

All notifications

Show battery percentage

- Swipe down the notification panel twice
- Tap on the three dots
- Select status bar

- Toggle on the show battery percentage

Activate landscape mode

This feature will allow you to work in landscape on your Samsung s20 series. To activate this feature, long-press your home screen wallpaper as you did earlier,

Rotate to landscape mode
Rotate the Home screen automatically when your phone's orientation changes

scroll down and look for rotate to landscape mode. Toggle on this option to enable it. Now when you turn your phone horizontally, the layout of your phone shows a landscape display , and when you toggle off, it disables the feature.

Switch off Samsung daily

To the left of your home screen is a field called **Samsung daily**. It is full of all kinds of areas from news media and other services.

To switch it off, long press on the home screen wallpaper and then swipe to the right then toggle off to switch off Samsung daily.

Toggle on to activate Samsung daily.

Swipe down notification anywhere

These allow you to access your notifications and tiles bar quickly and efficiently, considering the display size of the phone.

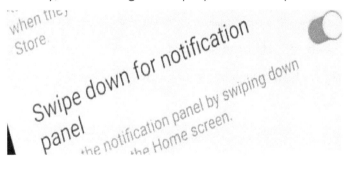

Go back to your home screen settings by long-pressing the home screen wallpaper and tap the home screen settings option. Scroll down and tap on swipe down for notification settings. Now, the notification panel shows whenever you swipe down anywhere on the home screen.

All apps on the home screen

So, if you draw all your applications on the home screen, all apps will be seen on different docks after the first dock is fully depending on how numerous your applications are.

You can access these settings on the home screen just choose home
screen layout and then select Home screen only
and all your apps will be spread across over the home screen
rather than in the app drawer.

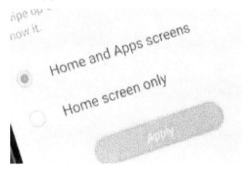

If you are using the app draw, you can alphabetize your apps.

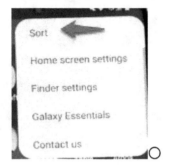

Open the app drawer and tap on the little dots on the top corner
to open the menu.

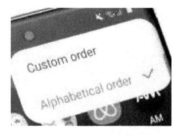

Tap sort, and you can choose alphabetical order, and all your apps
will automatically sort themselves out alphabetically.

Tap to show a fingerprint scanner

You can have your fingerprint icon to illuminate while your phone is sleep and lock by tapping your phone to know where it is to unlock it.

Head into settings, scroll down and tap on biometrics and security, then the fingerprint. Type in your pin or password and head to show the icon when the screen is off. Tap on this, and you have these three options

- **On always ON display**
- **Tap to show**
- **None**

Select tap to show to activate this feature.

Refresh rate and Quad HD

resolution

By default, the Samsung display is set to 60Hz. But if you want a high refresh rate for all to smooth and animation rate, go to settings, display, motion smoothness, then chooses 120Hz.

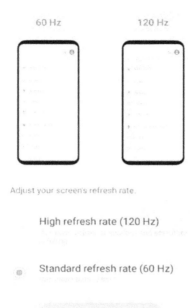

60 Hz   120 Hz

Adjust your screen's refresh rate.

High refresh rate (120 Hz)

Standard refresh rate (60 Hz)

You can only choose this if the screen resolution is set to FHD.

To access the screen resolution settings, head to settings, display then screen resolution, and select WQHD+. Samsung default resolution is FHD+, which hinders having smoothness and refresh rate of 120Hz.

Enabling Quad HD resolution is ok if you are on s20, but on the plus and Ultra, you might not want to show up the experience.

Select a resolution. Some currently running
apps may close when you change the
resolution.

HD+   **FHD+**   WQHD+

1600 × 720   **2400 x 1080**   3200 × 1440

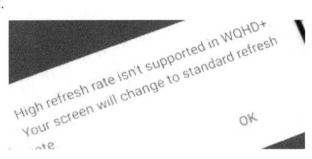

As soon as you choose the WQHD+, it will switch the refresh rate
to 60Hz.

High refresh rate isn't supported in WQHD+.
Your screen will change to standard refresh

OK

It is quite complicated to select out of smoothness and screen
resolution.

Chapter 7

Device security

Lock screen setup

Samsung s20 series is the most secured device the company has ever made is the first to feature a new secured processor called THE GORDON SHAPE to protect against horrible tasks similar to the google is being put in the pixel phones.

In other to set up your lock screen, swipe down on the screen and tap on Settings, scroll down and tap on the lock screen to select the lock screen type. Under this, you will see the following options

- **Swipe:** When you select this as your lock screen type, you only need just a swipe on your phone screen to unlock it. It is not advisable to use this type of lock screen due to no form of security in it.

- **Pattern:** This type of lock screen is widespread on Android devices.

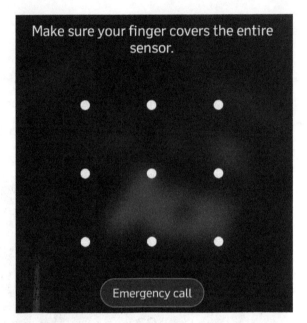

It is a form of lock screen in which you have to secure your phone by making a line drawn on targeted areas.

- **Pin:** A pin is a form of security lock that has to do with digits. Back then,

it comprises of only four-digit numbers, and with vast in technology, you can add up to twelve-digit numbers. To input your pin, swipe up on the lock screen.

- **Note:** If you select this action, you will access your home screen immediately when you press the side key.

Activate face unlock recognition

Even though the Galaxy N20 modules don't feature dedicated sensors on the front for facial scanning, they still have the options for face recognition. Face unlock security is more even convenient and is just a feature you should only be aware of because technically, this doesn't have any 3D depth sensor which isn't as secure as face ID.

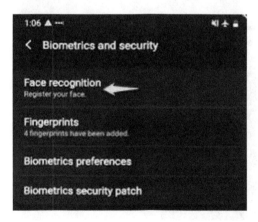

To enable this feature, what you are going to do is go into your settings, check biometric and security, then tap on it, tap on face recognition, input your pin, then tap continue.

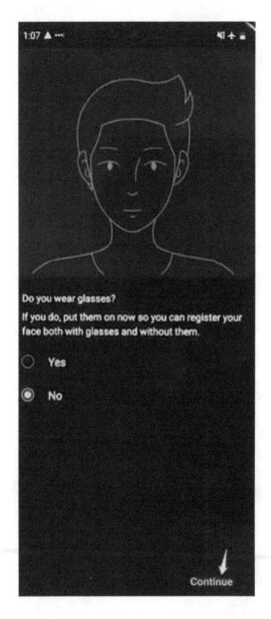

Do you wear glasses?

If you do, put them on now so you can register your face both with glasses and without them.

○ Yes

◉ No

Continue

If you wear glasses, tick YES, then put on the glasses to register your faces with glasses or without them, and if you don't do wear glasses, tick NO to record only your bare face. Tap on continue, wait some seconds to register your face, then click done.

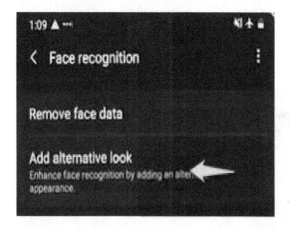

From there, you can add an alternative lock that will help if you have someone else that might need to get into your phone like your significant other or maybe a relative. You can scan their face, and then they can get into your phone using face recognition. Ones all these are enabled, make sure face unlock is on, or it should automatically turn on itself. If it happens, you wear glasses one day or sometimes a wig; you can scan your identity using those things as well so that it will recognize you.

Fix fingerprint issue

If you are having a tough time with your fingerprint scanner, follow these few recommendations that might work for you, and improve your usability.

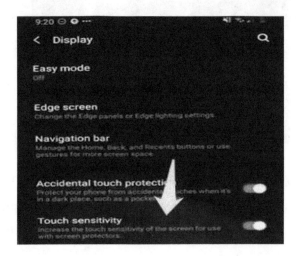

After every big system update, make sure you delete your current fingerprint and re-adjustable them.

Increase touch sensitivity if you are using a third-party screen protector (settings, display, touch sensitivity)

Register the phone fingerprint multiple time and try to avoid repeating the same path each time you register.

Google play protect

Google implemented google play protect while back to help avoid more malware and other harmful applications installed on the device. Generally speaking, Google protects works in the background as you download apps, but you can majorly scan your system if you want to.

To enjoy this feature, all you need is go to settings, tap on biometric and security and then tap on google play protect. You can also use the search bar in the settings to navigate this feature.

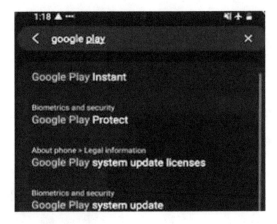

Just type google play protect, tap on it and then tap on google play protect again, and later on the next interface, you tap on the settings logo at the top right corner.

Over there, we have two different settings Scan apps with play protect, Improve harmful apps protection. To do a system scan and check the condition of your apps, refresh with the logo beside "looks good."

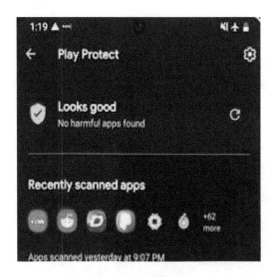

Samsung pass

If you are looking for a free pass manager that fast in secure, Samsung pass is excellent. It manages your passport, payment information, all secured by fingerprint and face authentication, but unfortunately, there is no desktop in the front, but I can figure how to access it.

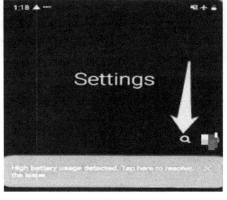

Bounce into the settings, and tap on the search icon, search for Samsung pass. Over there, there are three options one for fingerprint, one for face recognition, and the last for biometric and security.

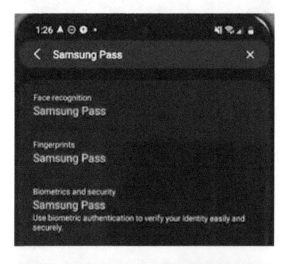

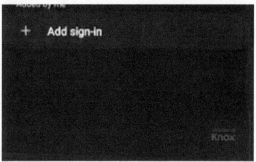

Tap on the one under biometric and security, then tap on Samsung pass again. Setup your Samsung pass and add sign in details of websites or applications you wish to use Samsung pass to access.

Tap on the three dots to go into the settings to activate the biometric to authenticate Samsung pass identity.

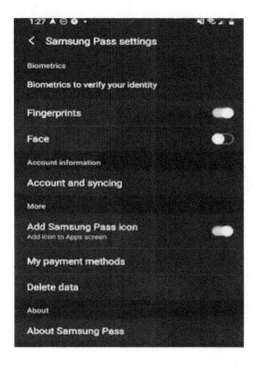

The fingerprint is registered as soon as you register. Under this, you can add the Samsung app icon to your desktop and app screen. You can also add a payment method to your Samsung, and of course, you can delete all of your Samsung pass data.

Samsung blockchain Keystore

Samsung has been using the combination of hardware and software android devices for security purposes known as KNOX.

It is no more news; they've been using it for years; however, add somewhat new features within the settings called Samsung BLOCKCHAIN KEYSTORE. It's meant to be for professional business investors and other people that might be venturing into cryptocurrency.

Another way to go into the device search without going into the settings is to pull up your app drawer, tap on search, and input blockchain. It is just like it does when you search from settings.

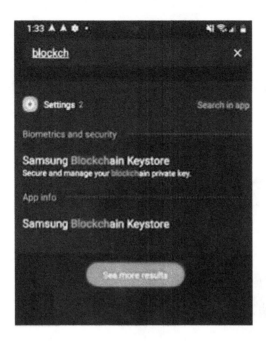

It might save you a little bit of time, but I just want to teach you both ways. Tap on Samsung blockchain Keystore, tap on it again, then agree and continue the setup.

You can either import an existing digital wallet that supports cryptocurrency or you create a new digital wallet.

Secure your folder

If you are having any documents, files, apps, or anything else on your phone you want to keep private, then you should probably check out the secure folder. It allows you to store things and set up a folder, and in other to gain access to the content, you need to verify your identity through either biometrics or maybe an account password. Best of all, if you log in to your Samsung cloud account on your laptop or desktop computer, you gain access to everything stored within that folder.

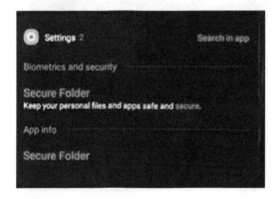

In other to turn on the secure folder, go ahead to the search bar and then type in a secure folder, tap secure folder under settings then tap secured folder again, pick a verification method to use, tap on next, input your selected identity, tap continue and do it one more time for verification.

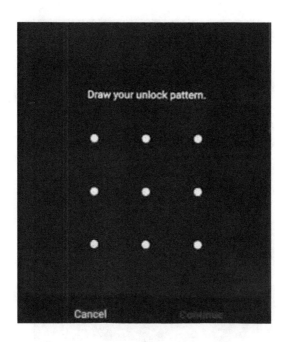

By default, it will store your gallery, calendar events, contacts, camera, internet (browsed history, passwords, etc.), my files, and Samsung notes. You can also add various apps, including third-party apps, to your secure folder.

You can also add different files, including images, videos, audio, documents, and my files (browse your file structure and find different things like your download folder, etc.)

Secure Wi-Fi

Here is another cool security feature. Samsung equips all of its phones with the settings known SECURE WI-FI, a glorify VPN, but you get it for free.

Go ahead and search for secure Wi-Fi from your search bar, tap on the option under settings, tap on secure Wi-Fi one more time, and take you to your account page.

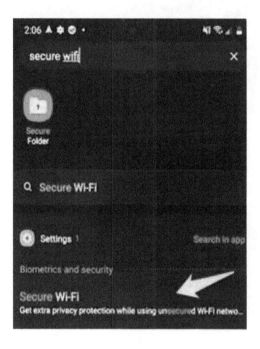

Here, you can either upgrade your account to get more data. Tap on "protect" to run the VPN. You can check your protection plan; this is where you upgrade your account. You can also check on your protected apps, which can be enabled or disable and also check on your protection history.

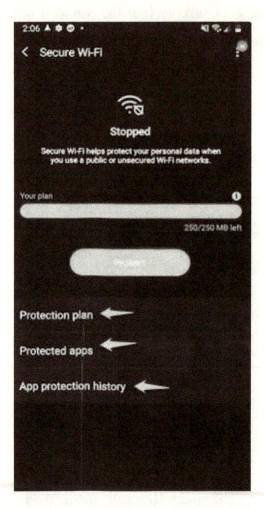

There are other settings you need to be aware of. Tap on the three dots in the top right corner.

Auto protect Wi-Fi: You can have it automatically turn ON whenever you connect to any Wi-Fi networks

Trusted Wi-Fi networks: you can customize its experience by trusting some Wi-Fi networks while not trusting others.

Use location information: This enables us to use or block location information.

Show icon on the home screen: Enable this to have access to secure Wi-Fi on the home screen quickly.

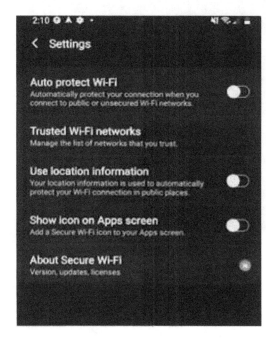

Encrypt and Decrypt Sound Disk Card

Samsung makes it possible to encrypt and decrypt your SD card, which you have or have not to store any vital information on it.

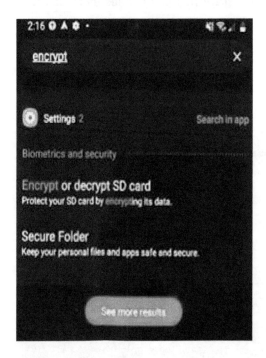

Head into the search bar and search for "encrypt," tap on it, a brief explanation on the feature is shown. Take a moment to read the information, then tap on encrypt SD.

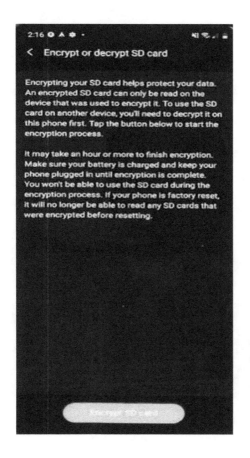

If another way round, you want to decrypt your SD card, follow the same procedures, and tap on decrypt SD.

Pin windows (child mode)

If you are a parent and you do attend to occasional, which facilitates giving your phone to kids to play with or watch movies while you take care of some grown full business, you are going to love to pin windows. It is super useful and will protect your kid from wandering places on your phone that he/she shouldn't avoid getting anything useful accidentally deleted.

Go ahead and do a search for pin window from your search bar, tap on the pin window, then toggle it to ON pin window.

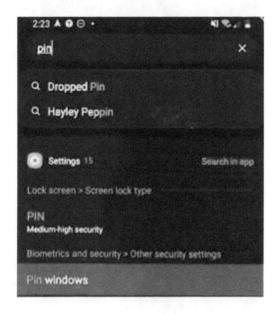

To check pin window application, go to the recent apps, tap on the app icon you wish to allow pin window, tap on pin this app, a pop-up will come up, tap "ok," and the app would be pinned.

The only way to get out of the app is to swipe up and hold the pinned app, and the phone will lock then unlock to leave the app.

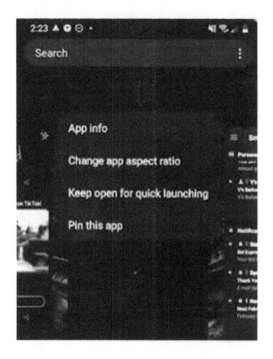

Customize your app permission

Sometimes the app you are using might gain access to something on your phone that is questionable. For example, maybe you download the podcaster app without knowing better, you give information to use the cameras. Many didn't know this information can be changed after you have downloaded the app and then agreed to everything.

Go to the search bar and search for permissions, and right there, you have a location for app permissions, app permission manager, and then privacy permission manager.

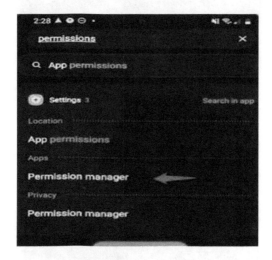

Tap on app permission manager, and you have all of the different permissions that you have on your phone such as;

- ➢ Body sensor
- ➢ call log
- ➢ camera
- ➢ contacts
- ➢ location
- ➢ microphone
- ➢ phone
- ➢ physical activity
- ➢ SMS

- ➢ Storage
- ➢ Additional permission
  - o Car information
  - o Read instant messages
  - o Write instant messages

You can just go through, say you tap on the camera, and check what apps you can use your camera.

Disable any app that you found a little bit suspicious, and you don't want them to have access to your camera.

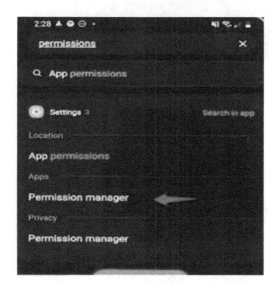

Go back to permission under the location you can do the same thing.

Check what apps are using your location services, and again, if you feel that app should not have access to that information, just turn it off.

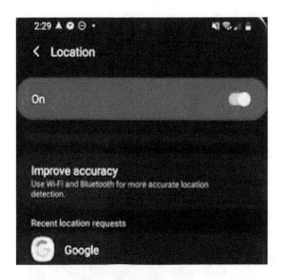

Personalize your contents

Here is a huge deal, but if you are sketchy about Google, Samsung, and everyone in between knowing your location, your likes, and dislikes, etc. disabling customization services might help you sleep a little bit better at night.

Customization services allowed Goggle and Samsung to use your personal information, whether through your used pardons, location, call history and to the voice services and deliver customs ads app in another suggestion base after that information.

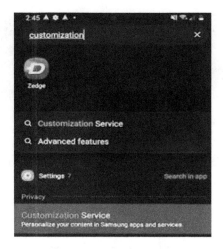

Go ahead to the search bar and search customization, tap on "customization service," tap on "customization service" one more.

By default, it may, and it may not be automatically turn on just depends on what you enabled while during the setup process. If It is already turned on, disable customization service, customization ads, and marketing will turn off all devices. Tap on turn off o the pop-up.

Now the customization service is completely turn off.

Clear your customization service log

If you choose to disable the services and they are ON by default. What you are going to do is go back to the customization service, tap on erase personal data, tap on erase, and verify your identity.

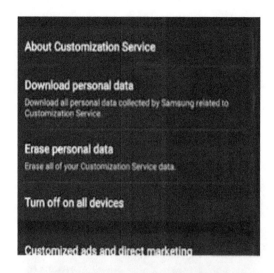

Trusted devices to unlock

If you tend to use several Bluetooth devices throughout the day like the watch, headphones, etc. you may be looking into trusted devices that might save you a little bit of time when it comes to getting inside your phone. You can make any device connected to your phone trusted devices, which simply means when your phone is connected to that specific device, you can unlock your phone without the need to verify your ID.

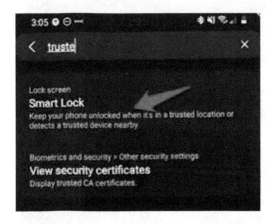

Typically, by default, when you connect a Bluetooth device, you get a notification asking you if you want to trust the tool. Just in case it doesn't happen to you, go into the settings and do a search for trusted devices, tap on it and tap on the smart lock again, enter your pin, tap on trusted devices, tap on add trusted device, and you pick the device you want to trust then tap "add" on the pop-up.

Add a trusted device

Add a trusted Bluetooth device to keep this device unlocked when connected.

ADD TRUSTED DEVICE

119

Trusted places

Another way of getting in your phone a little bit faster is by using trusted places. What you do is to assign a specific location within the settings. Whenever your phone gets into the vicinity of that location, you no longer require to input your passcode or your fingerprint.

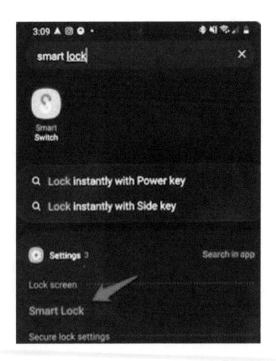

Just like trusted devices, a trusted location is also under smart lock. Go to the search bar, and search for "smart lock," tap on smart lock under the lock screen settings, tap on the smart lock again, input your pin if activated, tap on trusted places, tap on your present location, then update to add as trusted place. It will automatically pick the location of your current place.

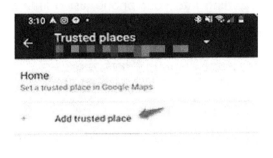

On-body protection

The last way of getting into your phone just a little bit quicker is enabling on-body detection.

These allow your phone sensor to detect if your phone is in your purse, pocket, backpack, bag. If it detects these things, then you are not required to enter any passcode or verification to get inside your phone. You are speeding up the process a little bit.

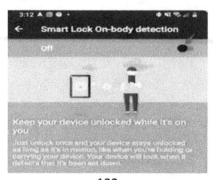

Just like trusted devices and trusted places, on-body detection is also under the smart lock section. Just go through the previous procedures, tap on-body detection, toggle ON, tap Continue on the pop-up.

Chapter 8

Find my device

Some may not know this is a way to track your device within the settings. Enabling allows you to track your device and perform other options if you lost your phone or stolen.

To activate this feature, go into settings, tap on biometric and security, locate "find my mobile" and tap on it, and you have the option to find my mobile and turn it ON.

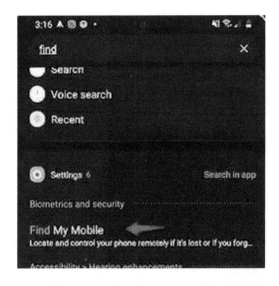

You can also access this feature if you go into your search bar and do a search for "find my mobile," tap on "find my mobile," and you are good to go.

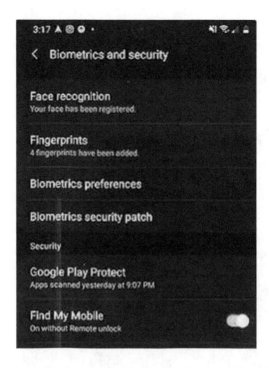

When you tap on "find my mobile," you have a couple of other settings such as

Remote unlock: This a great feature, in case you forget your pin or password, you will able to unlock your phone remotely and access the same Samsung without losing any of your data. Do enable it.

Send the last location: This is a good one in case you lost your device or stolen. Do enable it.

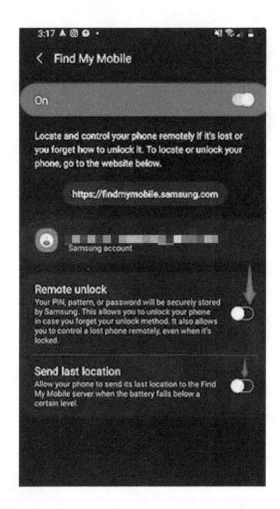

Add contact information on the lock screen

In case you lost your phone, and someone finds it and doesn't know who to contact because the device will be lockdown and the founder will not be able to get inside of it.

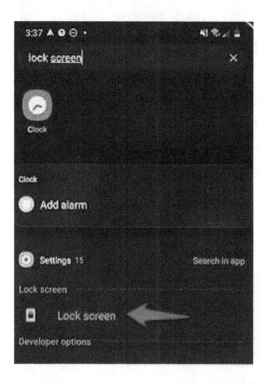

Go into your search bar and do a search for lock screen, then tap on it, scroll down to contact information and do a tap on it and then write the information you want it to display on the lock screen.

May be for example, "if lost contact xxx-xxx-xxxx." Add a contact that is saved for them to call in other to get in contact with you.

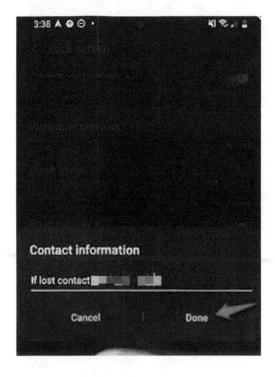

Secure lock settings

Secure lock settings is an essential feature for protecting your phone data against someone who stole your phone. This feature can have your phone automatically perform a reset after 15 incorrect login attempts.

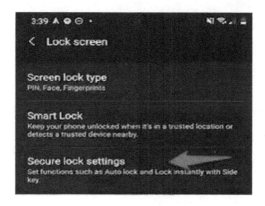

To set it up, go back into the lock screen settings, and ten locate secure lock settings and tap on it, input your ID if activated, and here you have the option for auto factory reset, tap on it to enable it.

Chapter 9

Wi-Fi calling

Wi-Fi calling enables you to receive or make calls over a wireless internet connection. It doesn't undergo a traditional telecommunication provider. If you are in an area where the usual calling network is weak or unavailable, Wi-Fi calling is an alternative to make voice calls.

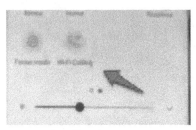

To activate or enable Wi-Fi calling on your N20 series is quite simple and amazing. The method to activate this feature is the same for all modules ranging from the N20 regular to the N20 Ultra.

All you need is your N20 with a sim card installed from a service provider that supports it, something like AT&T, T-Mobile, Verizon.

Connect your phone over a Wi-Fi, and you don't need to go much into the settings swipe down to the notification tiles panel, swipe left to locate the Wi-Fi calling logo, toggle it on, and response to the pop-up with turn on.

Depending on whether it is time to use it, you will see the calling symbol next to the Wi-Fi icon, but don't worry, you may not see it there, but Wi-Fi calling is activated.

Here is another method to activate Wi-Fi calling.

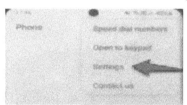

Go to the phone app, tap the three vertical dots at the right top corner, tap on Settings, scroll down, and here you have Wi-Fi calling to enable.

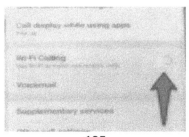

Chapter 10

Advanced features of the N20 series

Now let's dive into the advanced features of the Samsung galaxy s20 series. The very first thing you are to do is swipe down to the notification panel, click on the settings/logo at the top right corner. Or you look for the settings application, allow the phone to show the settings interface, scroll down, and you will see the advance features tap on it.

Under this, there are lots of features we will be looking into in this chapter. Mind you, some features such as; **Bixby Routine, Call & text on other devices, Link to Windows** will be discussed in detail in another chapter.

Double press

To activate these features, enable the double press option.

After you might have tapped on advanced features, tap on the side key, which is the single key on the side. Of course, the side key means the single access known as the power button.

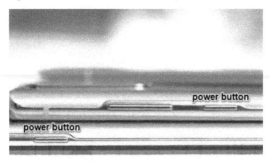

On the norm, if you press the key just one-time, it locks the screen. If you double press the button, it will launch an application, or you can choose to start the quick launch camera. So basically, you can just double-tap the button and boom! The camera launches, and that's great for a quick shot. Some people like Bixby, so if you select open Bixby and double press the button, it will launch the Bixby application. We are going to discuss in detail **"what is Bixby?"** in its chapter.

There is another option under the double press, which is unique. If you use an application often, you can quickly access the application if you select an open app option, and you double press the side key.

To select and save an app, tap the settings ✿ logo beside open app, and select.

Press and hold

Alright, if you press and hold the side key, you can wake up Bixby, or you can alternate the power off menu. So, if you press and hold the side key, it will show the power off menu interface. If you select wake Bixby and press and hold the side key, it will open the Bixby application.

"If you select wake Bixby, how will you going to power off your phone.?"

NOTE: *When you swipe down to the notification panel, there is a power logo* ⏻ *beside the settings logo* ⚙ *. Press it to show the power off the interface. Furthermore, you can only disable double press if you don't want to use it.*

Screenshot and screen recorder

It is such a fantastic feature where you can either take a screenshot or record the screen.

Under this section, we have;

Screenshot toolbar

So, every time you take a screenshot by pressing the power button and the volume down, it will give a screenshot and a screenshot toolbar below

Where all these features on the toolbar allow you to edit the screenshot on the go, screenshot the full information on a page at a time, tap on this icon ⚙ and it will be saved in your gallery. If you like to add a hashtag to your screenshot, you can get this done by tapping this logo # . If you want to crop or draw on your screenshot, kindly tap this logo ⟲ . Another feature of this screenshot toolbar is that you can share your screenshot instantly and delete automatically after it has been shared. To do this, tap on this logo .

You can also select the format you want your screenshot to be saved. We have the JPG, which is the most accessible format and most shareable format in the world, and the PNG.

Screen recorder settings

With this, you can record the screen of the device when you tap on it. You will have all the settings under it.

If you select no sound, you will record the screen with no sound. Still, if you choose media sound, the screen will record media audio on the phone, or if you select the last option, which is media sound and mic, it will pick your voice or any external voice outside around the phone.

There are also options for you to select the video quality of your choice. We have the **1080p, 720p and 480p.**

To record the screen, swipe down to the notification panel and here you will see the screen recorder logo enable it, then you click allow for anything they ask for, and then you choose from the sound options, the press starts recording. It will countdown three then after, and the screen record will start. You will notice a toolbar on the screen which is not visible in the record. To stop the screen record, do tap on this logo and the file is saved to your gallery. Go to your gallery and check screen recording to view your saved work.

Motion and gestures

Lift to wake up

This feature allows your device to wake up whenever it is lifted. If you enable this feature, your device will wake up automatically when lifting.

Double-tap to wake

This feature has been in android devices for some years. If you have this enabled, whenever you double-tap on the screen, it will come up

Smart stay

The smart key keeps the screen on while you're looking at it. If you enable this feature, your screen will be on while starring at it until you are done looking at it.

Smart alert

The smart alert is another fantastic feature that gives feedback on the notification(s). If your phone screen is turned over down and you have missed notification(s), it will vibrate when lifting a little bit, but if it doesn't vibrate, it shows no missed notification.

Easy mute

If somebody calls you or the alarm goes off, you can mute 🔕 by placing your Hand over the screen or turn the screen face down.

Palm swipe to capture

With this feature, you can take a screenshot by swiping over the screen. It will save the stress of using the buttons feature. Mind you; this feature will also work while the keyboard is available.

Swipe to call/send messages

Swipe to call/send messages allows you to make calls when you swipe right on contact and enables you to send a message when you swipe left. This feature is fantastic.

One-handed mode

Another impressive feature is the one-handed mode. It allows you to scale under the display size to use the phone with one hand. This feature is of two types; we have the button version, which is applicable when you double-tap the home button. It will make the screen smaller, which is easier to manage with one hand. If you have a small hand, you can resize it to your satisfaction when you press and drag from the edge of the resized screen. To disable one-handed mode, tap on the black field. To use the gesture version, press and swipe down on the home button. To move it side to side, tap on this logo .

Dual messengers or applications

This feature offers you to have two messenger applications because every app deserves its data. You can have two separate accounts on Facebook, WhatsApp, and a lot of other messenger apps. Supported apps will be shown, and you enable it. It helps to operate two accounts at a go.

File transfer made easy

File transfer is another fantastic feature of the Samsung galaxy s20 series; tap on it to enable it.

What happen is let assume you want to share something with anybody from your gallery, locate the picture or video, press and hold, tap on share and if anybody is available for quick share is going to show right over here.

1 item
8:03 AM

Quick Share

Share instantly with people nearby. On the other person's device, make sure that Quick Share is turned on in the quick panel. **Tips**

Ensure there is a nearby other Samsung device, and a quick share is also enabled on it. This feature will allow you to share large files instantaneously while over your WI-FI connection.

144

Send SOS messages

Emergency message Is a vital feature if you want to make sure you are getting to take care of in case of an emergency. It could be anything, or somebody wants to bump on you. It can be used to send a quick message to a contact that you know will take action. So, what you do is to enable this and agree on the terms. Once you have allowed it, you have to add at least one recipient to send an SOS message. Click on add and create a contact then save it. Now, if you press the side-key three times quickly, the phone will take photos of your current situation with the front and back camera and also record an audio voice of your surroundings for 5-10 secs and send it through your emergency contact

NOTE: *You can add multiple contacts*

Access your phone on your computer

This feature is effortless to activate. All you need is a window system (computer). If you enable this, you will be prompt to go to your windows PC download an application, and you will be able to project the entire form on to your window display. It's a susceptible feature but very easy to use. Connect your phone to your computer so that you can access your texts, notifications, recent photos, and more

When you enable this, it will ask you to log in to your Microsoft account

NOTE: *This doesn't work with mac as of this writing*

Floating notifications

Floating notification is also an advanced feature that allows you to reply to notification(s) in a pop-up window. Whenever you received a notification, let assume an SMS the smart pop-up will be displayed on your screen. When you tap, it is going to expand, and you can respond as you please. You can also move it around like a window when you hold on its drag. You can also resize it to your satisfaction. It can also be minimized by tapping this logo and maximize with this logo . It can be enabled for various apps base on your needs.

NOTE: *This is only available for apps that support multi-window.*

Access your Calls and texts on other devices

Here is another similar feature but only works with other Samsung devices. You can call and text on other devices that also support this feature. As long you are logged in with the same Samsung account when your phone rings, the tablet will ring as well, and take a call and respond to a text on that other device, and they will be linked together using your Samsung account.

Chapter 11

———◦———

Bixby

Automate tasks with Bixby routine

Bixby routines are "IF" and "ELSE" statements, so basically, if you need a condition on your phone meets a condition, your phone performs several functions that you defined. For example, we have some presets, let's tap on Good morning preset. You will see "if" the time is equal to 9 am (you set your preferred time), what you are to do is you tap on next "then" you want your phone to perform this functions, and again, all these functions can be removed, or you can add functions as you pleased.

Remember, because the Bixby routine is automated, they only run when the condition is met. You don't have to do anything; they run automatically in the background.

If you tap on this logo ⋮ at the top right corner, you see how to use it. When you swipe down to the notification panel, it will tell you this routine is running right now.

You can also go to settings to configure the followings;

- **Samsung Account**
- **Show Bixby Routine icon**
- **Customization Service and**
- **About Bixby Routine**

Activate Bixby quick command

Bixby quick comment is a single action or set of activities that can be activated with a word or a phrase. To access Bixby quick command, you are going to go inside the Bixby app and make sure it is enabled, but if you disabled Bixby, then you are not going to see inside the app. Another way to access Bixby is by using the start launcher. Swipe to the left on the home screen, there is Bixby voice pen as a card, tap on more, and it will take you to the same page then tap on the three dots right here and tap on quick command, and you will have two options name; Recommended & My commands.

Recommended are other recommended quick commands based on different categories such as;

- productivity
- daily routine
- lifestyle and place.

My commands are the set of commands you currently have run, such as; the good morning command.

The quick command may not be for everybody, and this is just the stock recommended good morning quick command; and if you want to customize it to suit your satisfaction, there are a couple of ways it can be done.

The first one is to tap on the good morning, which is the stock command. From there, you can remove and add commands.

Another method is by tapping on the three dots and tap delete to remove the stock commands, tap on recommended go on daily routine, tap on a good morning, then tap on edit. Now you can start taking away or add different actions to take place whenever you say good morning. Tap on done to save your command.

So, that's a quick look at Bixby's quick commands. There are also extremely useful for smart home control, especially if you use Samsung appliances or tie in smart things.

Extract text with Bixby vision

You can access Bixby's vision in two different ways.

The first one is to open the camera and tap on the settings logo
at the left upper corner and launch Bixby vision.

The second one is using voice to open Bixby's vision through this command. Hey, Bixby, "open Bixby vision." Hold the side key and say the command.

You can do several different things with Bixby's vision, including identifying objects, types of foods, plants, and stuff like that, but I will guide you on three other things I found slightly more practical.

One of its features is the ability to extract the text of an object. For example, you want to scan your business card, all you need is place the business card under your phone camera to be seen by the camera. Let Bixby vision scan it, and at the bottom, you can extract the text, tap on it and wait for some mins/secs for Bixby vision to extract the text.

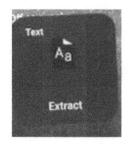

It is one of the most practical uses of Bixby's vision. To be able to store business card information and then store other contact information within your phone.

Bixby Vision for translation

Bixby Vision can also translate words inside of the main wall, road sign, business card, and kinds of stuff like that.

On the bottom left-hand corner, you have the translate logo

just tap on it; on the screen, you have Auto-English.

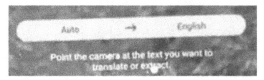

You can mainly go on and assign the language you want to translate. Place the phone on the text written on the object to translate while Bixby's vision is on. Within a couple of seconds, it will translate the text on the object.

It is super practical and sees you using it to get you around, especially when you travel abroad and you don't speak the language of the country.

Locate your location with Bixby vision

This feature can also help to pinpoint the location of a particular area, most notably when one is lost.

To use this feature, all you need is to go to the right-hand corner and tap on the location logo and point your phone straight down, and it is going to give you your location. There are also scan landmarks to identify where you are.

Isn't the most practical thing as you can pull up google map and that is going to pinpoint your location and probably more accurate than this, but it is still cool.

Control your camera with Bixby

You can also use Bixby to control your camera. The very first thing is to open your Bixby app, or you press and hold the side key if you have mapped it with the key. If you don't know how to get this done, endeavor to check the previous chapter.

Let's go through these examples.

Hey Bixby, "open the camera and take a picture with the rear camera."

It will take a picture using the rear camera.

Hey Bixby, "take a picture with the front camera."

It will get it done for you.

Hey Bixby, "start a video with the rear camera."

It will start recording the video using the rear camera just over my voice.

Hey Bixby, "take a live focus photo with the front camera."

I found this cool. You can pop your phone and put it on a tripod, and you control it with your voice.

You can access Bixby's vision in two different ways.

The first one is to open the camera and tap on the settings logo at the left upper corner and launch Bixby vision.

The second one uses voice to open Bixby's vision through this command "hey Bixby, open Bixby vision."

Chapter 12

Video & audio enhancement

Video and audio experience has to do with the best experience when you are watching movies or listening to music or watching videos on youtube.

To set this up, the first thing you have to do is go to settings, then to advanced features and scroll all away down to video enhancer and enable it. It enhances the video quality to enjoy brighter and more vivid colors. Supported apps are seen below, and as you download more, it will reflect.

You will do to make sure you get the best experience is to scroll up and go to sounds and vibrations, all away down to sounds quality and effects, then make sure DOLBY ATMOS sound is enabled. You can pick from the following options to change the sound effects.

- Auto
- Movie
- Music
- Voice

You can also manipulate these options from the notifications panel—all you have to do to hold on to this logo. When you tap on the logo, toggles to enable and disable function, but if you tap on the text, it will get to the quick button option. For the movie, hold the Dolby atmos logo, and it will show the quick button options for the movie.

Chapter 13

SIX essential applications

If you are new to android and especially the Samsung, there are five essential apps from Samsung that you must install on your new galaxy s20 series. These apps will just make your phone a lot easy and fun to use.

Video library

Let's talk about the first one. So, in your gallery, you may have a mix of photos and videos, and you know the galaxy N20 series contains excellent videos. Still, there is no way to segregate them fairly; they are all mixed, and there is no sort of filter or sorting available for you to just look at videos.

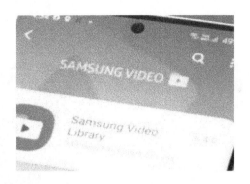

If you go to your Samsung galaxy store, not the play store, and search for a video library, you will get this app from Samsung. Once you installed it, you will be able to then see only videos in respective folders in your galleries. The photos are not visible anymore, just videos making see them in different views. And the best part is that it plays videos instantly and right upfront. Of course, you can change the orientation, you can switch to full-screen mode if you still want to see your dark area, but I think it is a great tool to just look at videos.

One Hand Operation+

You can set up your N20 series side gestures to go back, but if you long swipe, you get all your controls, but if you long swipe diagonally down, you will get your recent apps so you can quickly access them. You can swipe up diagonally to take a screenshot, or you can do the same on the Right Hand to go to your previous app. All of these are happening through this application called **One Hand Operation+**. You can configure the right edge and the left edge to perform certain activities that you generally do a lot of, and they are all just swiped away. Now you can configure one of these actions so you know what it straight right to do what a diagonal up and a diagonal down should do, and all of these options are available for you depending on what you are used to most you can configure.

Let's take a long swipe as an example.

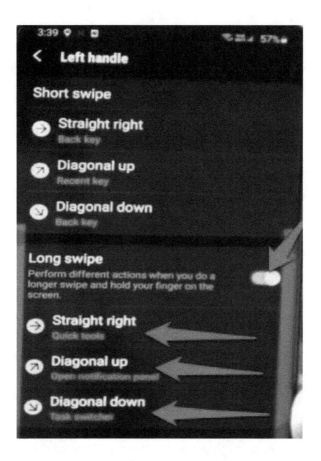

The first thing you have to do is to enable long swipe, and the swipe options will display underneath log swipe options. The swipe options are as follows;

- ❖ Straight right
- ❖ Diagonal up
- ❖ Diagonal down

If you swipe straight right, there are six options for you to select for the action to perform. This method applies to other options in the application.

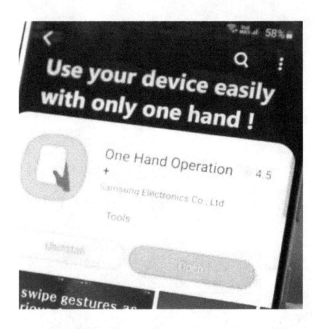

This application is available on the galaxy store and not the play store.

Samsung Email

Now the third one, funnily enough, Samsung doesn't include it need of Samsung email when the phone ships out to you.

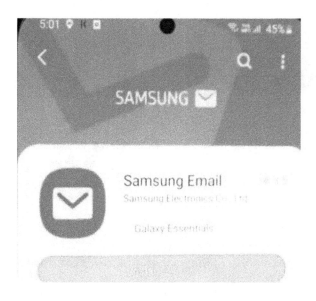

Now go to the galaxy store and download the Samsung Email app. It's one of the email clients that's been used out there. Though you might have a Gmail app, if you are looking for something more official like a professional email application, then Samsung email is a must. It's free and full of features. For example, if you change the phone

orientation and you open the application, all messages will be displayed in the landscape.

You will have a list style of view on the left and the reading pin on the left, just like you have it on your desktop, and also, you can resize the window depending on what you need it for.

The inbuilt search functionality is one of the best have ever seen.

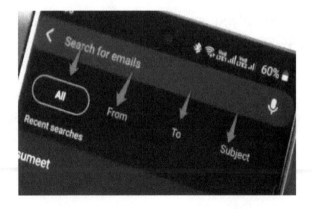

You can do your search just the way you do on the desktop.

You can search by all, from, to, and the subject line that makes it a lot easier to look for the email.

If you want to write your email, there are a couple of formats and options such as; **list, indentation, bullets, bold, italics,** and all available, which many other email clients do not provide.

Edge Lighting+

Your galaxy N20 series comes about 607 Edge Lighting style, but this application has got fluid, boomerang, and about 6 to 7 more that you probably do not have in your Edge Lighting effect.

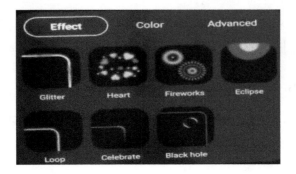

The effects are very cool. You can also set the transparency, width, and duration of your Edge Lighting. Go ahead to the galaxy store and search for Edge Lighting+

Sound Assistant

Now you probably have a much boring looking volume control panel than the one in the image below.

The equalizer settings can be changed without going into detailed sound settings, and you can also load any preset settings you have configured. So, all of these are happening right through this app called **Sound Assistant.** You can configure your volume control panel, and you can also change the color theme of the volume control panel, which is pretty cool.

There are also a couple of other settings, and for example, you can set individual app volume, so every time you open apps, you can preset the volume it should play at, which I think it's great flexibility to have. Also, you can have multi sounds, which means multiple apps together can play music and not just one specific app, which is the default from your system. It also enables us to have separate app sounds, for example,

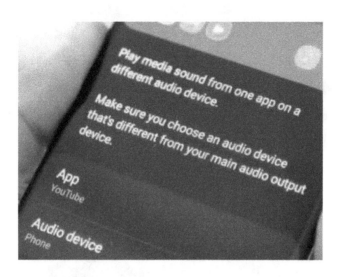

one app to play music in your earphone while another app can play through the phone's speaker system, which is very cool. To get this app, go to the galaxy store or play store and look for a sound assistant, and you will get this app.

Car mode

Car mode restricts the number of apps that you can use and changes the layout, so it's easier for you to use call while you are driving. You can increase the size of everything, so it's easier for you to tap. You don't have to be accurate, trying to focus more on the screen. It is just right here and easy to tap and move on.

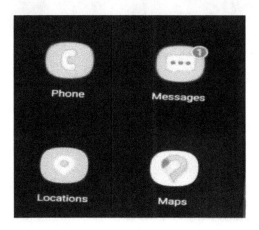

Now, a couple of things you can do is; first, you can restrict the notifications that come from application, and you can decide which apps and block incoming calls altogether. You can also re-arrange the apps that you have, isn't that a big deal. If you use the phone in landscape mode, you can select the navigation bar position. It depends whether you are driving on the left-side or right-side. The car mode automatically turns ON as soon as it detects you have connected to your car Bluetooth. The car mode automatically saves your parking location as early as you exit.

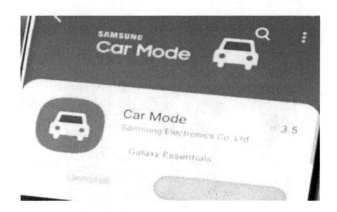

Overall, I think it is a pretty useful app. If you use your phone a lot for driving purposes,s go ahead and download from the galaxy store.

So, these are the six essential Samsung galaxy apps for your N20 series, and I think they are beneficial for you.

Chapter 14

How to optimize battery life

- **Enable dark mode:** The N20 series featured an AMOLED display, which consumes battery dues to its functionality. Enabling dark mode reduces battery consumption than the regular light mode.

  The dark mode can be schedule base on when you need it. Under this, you can also disable adaptive brightness.

- **Activate the standard refresh rate:** As you know, a high refresh rate facilitates battery consumption, and it gives more realistic animation and smoother scrolling. The standard refresh rate lasts longer than the battery.

- **Reduce screen resolution:** This device supports quad display, but the 120Hz refresh rate is only supported on FHD+. HD+ and FHD+ will reduce battery consumption.

- **Reduce screen timeout:** You can reduce the screen timeout to about 30 seconds to enhance battery life.

- **Disable Edge lightning/reduce apps support:** Whenever a notification comes up, there is a colorful light around the edge of the screen. You can disable edge lightning or minimize the number of apps to support this feature to reduce battery consumption.

- **Activate maximum power saving:** If you like playing games, obviously you will go for high performance, but the best option for the regular use is the optimized mode and minimum power-saving mode. But if you want extreme battery saving, you can go with the maximum power-saving mode. You can also enable adaptive power saving mode to set the power mode automatically based on your usage pattern.

- **Activate adaptive battery:** This will limit battery for apps you don't use.

- **Disable always-on display:** Always-on display allows the screen to sleep in a daydream. Notifications, clock, and date will be displayed when the screen is lock. Disable this to enjoy your battery life. This feature can also be scheduled.

- **Disable Samsung daily:** swipe your home screen to the right, toggle off to disable Samsung daily.

Chapter 15

The birth of the S pen

SAMSUNG S PEN
Galaxy Note

Samsung's first pen was introduced with the Galaxy Note in 2011. It was known a **phablet** because it came in a combination of a phone and tablet features. The S pen could detect 256 pressure points; it uses it quite limited. It was functioning as a pen, pencil, brush, and highlighter. It could also be used for navigation, taking a screenshot, handwriting, and touching the screen twice to open the S memo application.

SAMSUNG S PEN
Galaxy Note 2

The second S pen was completely redesigned by Samsung being longer back then and more organic, and it was able to detect 1024 pressure points. Among the new features of the S-Pen is the "Air view" feature that allows you to hover the pen over the top of an icon, email, or media to quickly glance at the preview without actually navigating away from the current screen. Another interesting feature was the" easy clip" that works by holding the S pen button. With the tip, one can quickly outline and crop content from virtually on the screen and then paste on the crops or email, note-taking, and image processing apps.

SAMSUNG S PEN
Galaxy Note 3

The S-Pen of Galaxy Note 3 has brought an improvement in terms of productivity features and handwriting. With air command, important features could be easily accessed, just like ejecting the S pen or pressing its button. Thus, with this function, it was easier to make calls, send emails or messages, and add others of note to the image captures. However, another interesting feature is S finder, which recognizes handwriting, and users could search for a memo base on the text.

SAMSUNG S PEN
Galaxy Note 4

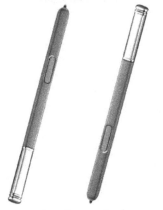

The S pen Galaxy Note 4 also had a major improvement in productivity tools, and the pressure sensitivity was doubled from 1024 to 2048 level. Small select, users could copy and paste text from a website or document—the S-pen behaving like a mouse for the first time. The S-pen "Photo Note" features allowed the stylus users to clip an individual portion of the photo and then copy more and share them with a few swipes

SAMSUNG S PEN
Galaxy Note 5

A very interesting thing the Galaxy Note 5 S pen could do is write directly on the phone screen even if it is turned off, the pdf writing function and scrolling screen capture. Simultaneously, the S-Pen could be ejected with a light push and no longer had to be removed manually, as in previous versions.

180

SAMSUNG S PEN
Galaxy Note 7

The Galaxy Note 7 S pen was able to detect a 4096 pressure point, and it was water resistance. Which means users can draw or write on the water or in the rain. It also has a new note-taking application screen write and small select. The most interesting was the animation select, which allowed users to create a 15seconds GIF by drawing a frame. The air command menu adds three more new features. Such as magnifier-the ability to zoom part of the screen up to 300%, glance-a commonly use the app for a tiny square which could be check at any time by hovering with the pen, and Google translates embedded in the S pen.

SAMSUNG S PEN
Galaxy Note 8

With the introduction of the Galaxy Note 8, Samsung has focused on improving the communication experience to be as fun as possible. So, the live message gave the users the ability to use the S pen to draw their animated GIF that can be shared with friends. Also, the translator could translate complex sentences and not individual words like the version on the Galaxy Note 7. However, the screen off memo allowed the users always to fix notes on the screen as reminders.

SAMSUNG S PEN
Galaxy Note 9

The Galaxy Note 9 S pen offered a wide range of note-taking and productivity and enhancing tools. It could be used remotely to photograph a group or control slides and presentation using the Bluetooth alley function. Also, the S-pen charges just 40seconds when docking to the phone. It lasts up to 200 clicks at times or 30mins on standby.

SAMSUNG S PEN
Galaxy Note 10

The S-Pen on the Galaxy Note 10 was like a little magic one. Users can control their phone remotely using simple gestures. For example, by pressing the S pen button, users can choose room or shooting modes, zoom the pictures, or access some functions with customizing gestures. Another interesting, useful feature was converting handwriting into text and exporting the file in a different format.

SAMSUNG S PEN
Galaxy Note 20

The Galaxy Note 20 S pen comes with many improvements and offers a realistic note-taking experience. Thanks to improving AI technology, a gyroscope sensor, and

an improved accelerometer. Also, latency has been reduced by almost 80% compared to the previous modules. Thus, giving the users a more realistic writing experience. In terms of gestures, Samsung has extended the controls to facilitate navigation on the phone regardless of application.

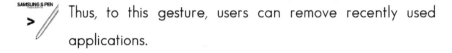 Thus, to this gesture, users can remove recently used applications.

This gesture redirects users back to the home screen.

This gesture means an action back.

This starts small select, and by moving the S stripe, it automatically activates the screen pen.

Chapter 16

S-Pen and its components

Activate S-pen proximity alert

The S-pen is a device for the Galaxy Note series to operate the device to replace fingers. The pen is such a device user can't do without because it makes it comfortable to use the device compare to the fingers. Though the S-pen has its housing as a human, we can easily forget it somewhere else's. With that, Samsung provides this feature called **proximity alert,** which notifies whenever the phone and the S-pen are far away in the distance. It means whenever it happens, you left or forget the S-pen somewhere else's it notifies, and you can easily get it back if you check your last location. With this feature enabled, the S-pen cannot be easily lost. It is a very useful feature.

Now, to activate this feature follow the steps below;

➢ Locate the **settings** on your phone and open it
➢ Scroll down to the **advance features** then tap on it
➢ Tap on **S-pen**
➢ Scroll down and locate **pen proximity alert**
➢ Toggle on it to activate the feature

To disable this feature, follow the same steps and toggle it off.

Unlock your device with S-pen

Nowadays, mobile devices can be unlocked in different ways. However, this feature is very new in android phones, most especially device with stylus pen like the S-pen you have with your Note 20 regular and Note 20 ultra has the upper hand to unlock the device with the pen. This feature was disabled by default meaning the user will need to activate it themselves. If this feature is enabled, you can easily unlock your device with the S-pen with just a click. Before you can enable this feature, if any of the standard security options are enabled, you will be asked to input it before enabling the S-pen unlock.

- Open the phone settings
- Got to the **advance features**
- Locate **S-pen** and select it
- Toggle on **S-pen unlock**; If you have any of the usual security locks enabled, input it to proceed
- Tap on **S-pen** then select **"Use S-pen to unlock"**

So, whenever you lock your phone, you can unlock with the S-pen by pressing the side key of the pen.

If you want to disable this feature, follow the same steps, and select **"Don't use"** in the last steps above.

Access the Note app anytime any moment

One of the benefits of the Note devices with stylus pen like the S-pen is using them to take note/memo down on the note app. Now, Samsung made it easy this time. As the note/memo is one of the prominent why there is an S-pen for the device, you can now take note/memo on the note app anytime at any moment. Be it your device is lock/sleep or while using another application. All you need is activate this feature, then press and hold the S-pen key and double tap on the screen to open the Note app. Mind you, and the S-pen nib must be closer to the screen while you perform this action, or it gives another result. Below is how you can get the feature activated.

- ➢ Open the phone **settings**
- ➢ Scroll down and select **advance features**
- ➢ Tap on **s-pen**
- ➢ Toggle on **screen off memo** and **create note with button** to activate the feature

If you wish to disable this feature, follow the same steps, and toggle off **screen off memo** and **create note with button.**

Preview item information

Over the years, Android devices can't preview information of files without pressing on details. Now, Samsung this time around came with this feature called **Air view** on the Note 20 series, which allows users to get little information when the S-pen is hovering on an item.

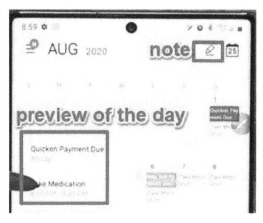

For example, on the calendar application, if you hover on a date, it gives the preview of what is happening on that, be it a public holiday or a remainder you configured to the date by yourself. Even while on the calendar, you can use the pen logo at the top right to create a note on the calendar and save it. If you go to the gallery and hover the S-pen on an image, it previews the image.

> ➤ Open the **phone settings**
> ➤ Got to the **advance features**
> ➤ Locate **S-pen** and select it

> ➤ Tap on **Air view** and toggle it on

If you want to disable this feature, follow the same steps, and toggle it off.

Enable/Disable S-pen pointer

While you hover the S-pen over the screen, there is a little pointer that moves around if it is enabled, which indicates where the S-Pen tip is pointing at a particular time. To disable this feature, follow the below steps.

> ➤ Open the **phone settings**
> ➤ Got to the **advance features**
> ➤ Locate **S-pen** and select it
> ➤ Toggle on **show pointer when hovering**

To enable this feature, follow the same steps and toggle it off.

Use multiple S-pen

If you have extra S-pen, maybe you've bought it due to backup if the one that came with the phone gets lost or stolen. This feature will simply help and allow us to use more than a pen on a device.

> ➤ Open the **phone settings**
> ➤ Got to the **advance features**
> ➤ Locate **S-pen** and select it
> ➤ Toggle on **allow multiple S-pen**

Customize what hold down the pen button do

The **S-pen button command** is part of the S-pen settings. It allows the pen to perform some customizable task when the side button is the press. For this feature to work very well, the S-pen should get farther away from the device. You can customize "if you hold down the S-pen button, what action do you want it to perform?".

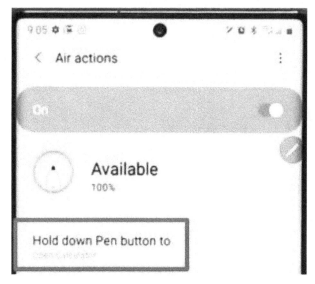

Almost all the S-pen features and apps are allowed to support this feature. Meaning, if you perform the action on the S-pen, it will open any of the apps you customized it to launch. Be it any of the

S-pen features or the camera, gallery, games, internet, chrome, office, and lot more. Here is how to go about the customization.

> - Open the **phone settings**
> - Got to the **advance features**
> - Locate **S-pen** and select it
> - Select **Air actions**
> - Toggle **on** to enable air action
> - To customize the app to launch; Tap on **hold down the pen button,** then select what app to open when the button is press.

Repeat these same procedures to change the app or disable this feature.

Customize anywhere air gesture actions

This feature is very similar to the previous one, but this time around, an air gesture is inclusive this time. The five (5) air gestures command is customized by default to enhance the control of the navbar, smart select, and screen white.

However, the air gesture command can be customized to suit your satisfaction.

➢ Open the **phone settings**

➢ Got to the **advance features**

➢ Locate **S-pen** and select it

➢ Select **Air actions**

➢ Toggle **on** to enable air actions

➢ To assign an action to the gesture; Tap on **any of the gesture and select another action**

➢ Toggle **on** the feature to enable it, then tap on any app to open when the button is press.

Repeat these same procedures to change the app or disable this feature. Keeps the pen a little bit farther away from the phone to work very well. Also, every single action there is customizable.

Customize apps air gesture actions

Apps air gesture actions are limited and not supported by all apps. This feature is more useful, and it enhances communication with apps to be so fast. This feature can be used to control apps from afar as long it is connected, and it doesn't void its supported distance length. It is more or less a remote control for the supported apps. Not everyone will be interested in controlling some apps with S-pen.

So, there is an option to disable apps you feel you don't need to control with S-pen. The action you want the app to perform is customizable.

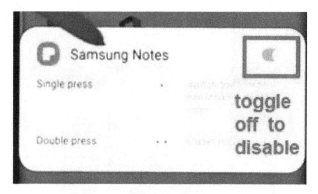

- ➢ Open the **phone settings**
- ➢ Got to the **advance features**
- ➢ Locate **S-pen** and select it
- ➢ Select **Air actions**
- ➢ Toggle **on** to enable air actions
- ➢ Tap **on** app then toggle **on** to enable or toggle **off** to disable the app

Air command menu-how to customize

The air command menu is an exclusive section of the S-pen, which is permanent on the Galaxy Note series. It is such a feature that gives quick access to the S-pen features. Such as create a note, smart select, write on the calendar, magnify, calendar, clock, PENUP, AR doodle, coloring, and so on. By default, the air command will open automatically if the S-pen is taken out of it housing. Also, you can customize this menu to the features and the app you use often.

At the top right corner is the battery connection of the S-pen, which indicates its battery percentage. The bottom left corner is the settings icon, which can also access the S-pen settings.

➤ Open-**air command** by taking the S-pen out of it housing

➤ Tap on the **Settings icon** in the bottom left corner

➤ Scroll down and tap on **shortcuts**

➤ Tap on **required apps or S-pen features** to add automatically to the list

➤ Tap on the **negative sign** "-" to remove an existing item from the air command

➤ Close settings once you are through with the customization

Enable/disable the air command floating icon

Maybe unconsciously, you do accidentally touch the air icon by mistake. Do not fret; the floating icon can be enabled or disabled from the settings.

> ➢ Open **settings**
> ➢ Scroll down and tap on **advance features**
> ➢ Tap on **S-pen**
> ➢ Scroll down to **show floating icon**
> ➢ **Toggle it off** to disable
> ➢ **Toggle it on** to enable

Know about air command menu features

 create note gives room to make new notes, edit notes, view notes, save notes, share notes, and sync your notes with other Samsung Galaxy devices. Notes saves will be seen in the Samsung notes app.

How to use:

 Smart select is a fantastic feature that enables you to clip, select any portion of the screen, and save it as a screenshot in your gallery. The selected portion is editable by writing on it with a pen, and it can be shared with friends.

 Screen white is quite similar to the smart select. But screen white captures the whole screen, and it can be edited with the pen tools, erase any edited errors, undo and redo and also share with other devices. The screen white serves as taking a screenshot with the pen. However, it can be customized under air gestures to take a screenshot with the assigned gesture.

 Live messages are the advanced version of smart select and white screen combine. This feature has to do with animation like drawing and writing what you have to say, then capture the process and convert it into GIF or emojis. The file saved from the live message can be shared with friends on social media.

 Translate is another remarkable feature of air command. This feature makes it easier for users to translate from one language to another.

How to use:

- ➤ Open the text you want to translate
- ➤ Open the air command menu
- ➤ Select translate
- ➤ Select your input language and the target language
- ➤ Hover on the text with the S-pen to translate word

- ➤ Tap the "T" logo to translate a paragraph

 for those that have a visual impairment or can't see very well, a magnifier is a feature

that allows you to zoom out a particular area on the screen where the S-pen hovers. The screen can be magnified up to 300%.

How to use:

> Open the air command menu
> Select magnify

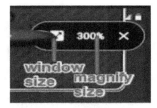

> Hover on the screen to magnify the area

 glance is another exciting feature. It allows you to glance at a minimized app while using another app. For example, you are jotting on the note from the browser. You can glance on the browser while the note app will not be closed.

How to use:

> Open the app to glance at
> Open the air command menu
> Select glance, the app you want to glance at is minimized to the right bottom corner is a small window

➤ Hover on the glance window to access the app

➤ To remove the glance window, press and hold on the
   window and drag to the delete icon on the screen

 With so many on your neck to take care,
it may be difficult to remember things in
days ahead. This feature helps to keep in
mind the activities ahead. You can write on your calendar and
saved it. Whenever you check your calendar, it serves as a
reminder.

How to use:

➤ Open the air command menu
➤ Select write on calendar
➤ Tap on the pen logo on the floating window to change
   the pen settings

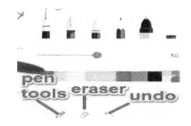

> ➢ Tap the eraser logo to erase

> ➢ Tap the undo logo to get last actions

> ➢ Tap the save at the top left corner to save as a note

Chapter 17

Samsung create note nine (9) tips

Quick note-taking

Samsung creates notes is a powerful air command feature for productivity and creativity. You can quickly take a note without unlocking your device. Just pop-out the S-pen from the bottom of your device and start writing on the screen. If the S-pen is already, press the pen button to activate the screen off memo and when you are through, tap save, and the note will be stored in the Samsung notes.

You can also access the Samsung note while your phone is unlocked from the shortcut menu by tapping the pen icon if it is enabled or you pull-out the S-pen from its housing then tap create the note.

Pen tools, highlighters & erasers

In the Samsung Note app, you can switch between the highlighters, pens, and erasers by tapping the icons in the toolbar. There are plenty of options to customize your pen thickness, type, and color.

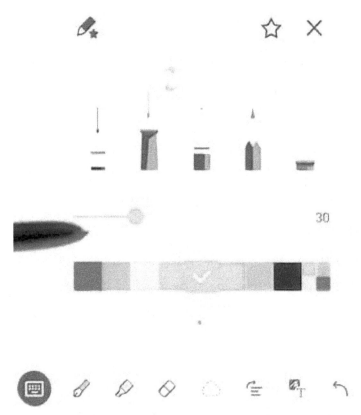

You can also erase things one stroke at a time, or you can go by area like a traditional eraser. To quickly access the eraser at any time, just hold the S-pen button.

Change the page template and background

Samsung made it possible for users to customize the type of paper they are writing on. First, tap the menu ⋮ icon and select page template.

<
Share

Save as file

Sort pages

Page template

Background color

Add to favorites

Add tags

Finger drawing on

You can also choose from various styles, including graph paper, wide, narrow lines, and to-do-lists. The background color could be changed to your personal touch.

Convert handwriting to text

You can change the handwriting note to text note after. All that you have to do is to tap on the "T" icon to convert it into text. You can now copy that text into another app, or you convert the handwritten note right there.

Samsung note also recognizes emails and phone numbers. You can tap on the email or phone number written to reach out immediately.

Another great feature is that you can quickly straighten your note by tapping this straighten ⪚ icon.

Import PDF or image

Images and PDFs can be imported to the Samsung note app for further editing. To annotate an image or a PDF, just tap the paper click ⌀ icon; then, you can add a note right on the PDF or image.

You can also get an artist tech by embedding a PENUP drawing in your note.

Add a voice recording

You can add a live recording to your note to explain your idea verbally. When you are done, you can playback the recording and watch your sketch on the fold. It can be shared as a multimedia audio file.

Sort images

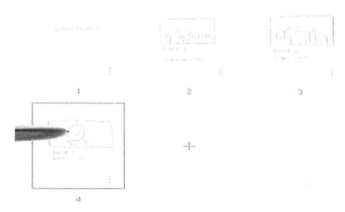

To reorder a multipage note, tap the menu ⋮ icon and select sort images. Now, long-press the page and drag it to its new position to reorder.

Save note in different file formats

Your notes can be saved in different file formats. To export your note, tap the ⋮ menu icon and select save as a file. You can choose to export as a PDF, Word, PowerPoint, image, or text.

Organize notes

A well organizes not the folder is the one that looks better. As you make use of the note app, you save several files to the folder with different names that are not in order. To keep things in order, you can organize notes from the home screen of the Samsung note app. Now, long press on a note to move it into a folder.

Books by the Author